ANNOUNCING TH
NOW IN PREPARA

The edition of *The Complete Works*

Volume I *Behold Your King:*
  The Complete Poetical Works of Frances Ridley Havergal

Volume II *Whose I Am and Whom I Serve:*
  Prose Works of Frances Ridley Havergal

Volume III *Loving Messages for the Little Ones:*
  Works for Children by Frances Ridley Havergal

Volume IV *Love for Love: Frances Ridley Havergal:*
  Memorials, Letters and Biographical Works

Volume V *Songs of Truth and Love:*
  Music by Frances Ridley Havergal and William Henry Havergal

David L. Chalkley, Editor   Dr. Glen T. Wegge, Music Editor

The Music of Frances Ridley Havergal by Glen T. Wegge, Ph.D.

This Companion Volume to the Havergal edition is a valuable presentation of F.R.H.'s extant scores. Except for a very few of her hymn scores published in hymnbooks, most or nearly all of F.R.H.'s scores have been very little—if any at all—seen, or even known of, for nearly a century. What a valuable body of music has been unknown for so long and is now made available to many. Dr. Wegge completed his Ph.D. in Music Theory at Indiana University at Bloomington, and his diligence and thoroughness in this volume are obvious. First an analysis of F.R.H.'s compositions is given, an essay that both addresses the most advanced musicians and also reaches those who are untrained in music; then all the extant scores that have been found are newly typeset, with complete texts for each score and extensive indices at the end of the book. This volume presents F.R.H.'s music in newly typeset scores diligently prepared by Dr. Wegge, and Volume V of the Havergal edition presents the scores in facsimile, the original 19th century scores. (The essay—a dissertation—analysing her scores is given the same both in this Companion Volume and in Volume V of the Havergal edition.)

Dr. Wegge is also preparing all of these scores for publication in performance folio editions.

This photograph of F.R.H. was taken by the photographers Elliott & Fry in London on Saturday, February 1, 1879, seven weeks after her 42nd birthday.

ROYAL BOUNTY;

OR,

EVENING THOUGHTS

FOR

The King's Guests.

BY

FRANCES RIDLEY HAVERGAL.

"That which Solomon gave her of his royal bounty."—1 Kings 10:13.

"Knowing her intense desire that Christ should be magnified, whether by her life or in her death, may it be to His glory that in these pages she, being dead, 'Yet speaketh!'"

Taken from the Edition of *The Complete Works of Frances Ridley Havergal.*
David L. Chalkley, Editor   Dr. Glen T. Wegge, Associate Editor
ISBN 978-1-937236-08-3   Library of Congress: 2011939759

Copyright © 2015 Frances Ridley Havergal Trust. All rights are reserved.
Frances Ridley Havergal Trust   P.O. Box 649   Kirksville, Missouri 63501

Book cover by Sherry Goodwin and David Carter.

"When I remember Thee upon my bed."   Psa. lxiii. 6.

Memory is never so busy as in the quiet time while we are waiting for sleep; and never, perhaps, are we more tempted to useless recollections and idle reveries than "in the night watches". Perhaps we have regretfully struggled against them, perhaps   2 Cor. x. 5. yielded to effortless indulgence in them,   Jer. iv. 14. and thought we could not help it, and were hardly responsible for "vain thoughts" at such   Psa. cxix. 113. times. But here is full help and bright hope. This night let us "remember Thee". We can only remember what we already know; oh praise Him then that we have material for memory! There is enough for all the wakeful nights of a life-time in the one word "Thee". It leads us straight to "His own self";   1 Pet. ii. 24. dwelling on that one word, faith, hope, and love, wake up and feed and grow. Then the holy remembrance, wrought by His   John xiv. 26. Spirit, widens. For "we will remember the   Psa. xx. 7. name of the Lord our God"; in its sweet   e.g. Ex. xxxiv. 5-7. and manifold revelations. "I will   Isa. ix. 6. remember the years" and "the works of   Psa. lxxvii. 10, 11. the Lord"; "surely I will remember Thy

The first page of a manuscript copy in F.R.H.'s handwriting of the Twenty-Seventh Day of Royal Bounty. See page 73.

CONTENTS.

DAY		PAGE
1.	The Royal Bounty.	1
2.	The Opened Treasure	4
3.	The King's Signature and Seal	6
4.	The Candour of Christ.	9
5.	From Death unto Life.	12
6.	Justified	15
7.	The Royal Wine.	18
8.	The Gift of Peace.	21
9.	The Abiding Joy.	23
10.	The Sure Afterward	26
11.	No Hurt	28
12.	The Putting Forth of the Sheep	30
13.	Safe Stepping	33
14.	Thine.	36
15.	Unto Thee for Ever	39
16.	Captive Thoughts.	42
17.	The Imagination of the Thoughts of the Heart	45
18.	The Everlasting Service.	48
19.	Most Blessed for Ever.	51
20.	Do Thou for Me.	54
21.	Marvellously helped	57

DAY		PAGE
22.	Thou understandest	60
23.	The Proof of His Purpose	62
24.	The Garnering of the Least Grain	65
25.	Vindication	68
26.	Wakeful Hours	71
27.	Midnight Rememberings	73
28.	The Bright Side of Growing Older	75
29.	The Earnests of More and More	78
30.	The Perpetual Presence	81
31.	The Fame-excelling Reality	84

LIST OF ILLUSTRATIONS

Frances Ridley Havergal, photograph portrait, 1879	ii
First page of manuscript of the Twenty-Seventh Day	iv
Part of Acts 27 in F.R.H.'s Bible	90

FIRST DAY.

The Royal Bounty.

"And King Solomon gave unto the queen of Sheba all her desire, whatsoever she asked, beside that which Solomon gave her of his royal bounty."—1 Kings 10:13.

Genesis 32:10	ALL God's goodness to us is humbling. The more He does for us, the more ready we are to say, "I am not worthy of the least of all the mercies, and of all the truth, which Thou hast shewed unto Thy servant." The weight of a great answer to prayer seems almost too much for us. The grace of it is "too wonderful" for us. It throws up in such startling relief the disproportion between our little, poor, feeble cry, and the great shining response of God's heart and hand, that we can only say: "Who am I, O Lord God, that Thou hast brought me hitherto? Is this the manner of man, O Lord God?"
Luke 5:8, 9	
Job 42:3	
2 Samuel 7:18–19	
Psalm 126:3 1 Kings 3:13	But it is more humbling still, when we stand face to face with great things which the Lord hath done for us and given us, which we never asked at all, never even thought of asking—royal bounty, with which not even a prayer had to do. It is so humbling to get a view of these, that Satan tries to set up a false humility to hinder us from standing still and considering how great things the Lord hath done for us; thus he also contrives to defraud our generous God of the glory due unto His name.
1 Samuel 12:7, 24	
Psalm 29:2	
	For, of course, we do not praise for what we will not recognise.
Isaiah 63:7 Psalm 68:19 Psalm 103:2	Let us try to baffle this device to-day, and give thanks for the overwhelming mercies for which we never asked. "Blessed be the Lord, who daily loadeth us with benefits." Just think of them deliberately (they are far too many to think of all in a flash); and how many did we actually ask for? Even that poor little claim was never brought to bear on thousands of them.

To begin at the beginning, we certainly did not ask Him to choose us in Christ Jesus before the world began, and to predestinate us to be conformed to the image of His Son. Was not that "royal bounty" indeed?

Then, we certainly did not ask Him to call us by His grace; for before that call we could not have wished, much less asked, for it. Then, who taught us to pray, and put into our entirely corrupt and sinful hearts any thought of asking Him for anything at all? Was not all this "royal bounty?"

Look back at our early prayers. Has He not more than granted them? did we even know how much He could do for us? did He not answer prayer by opening out new vistas of prayer before us, giving us grace to ask for more grace, faith to plead for more faith? Why, it is *all* "royal bounty" from beginning to end! And this is going on now, and will go on for ever, when He has brought us with gladness and rejoicing into His own palace. Not till then shall we understand about those riches of glory in Christ Jesus, out of which He is even now pouring out the supply of all our need.

The marginal reading is very beautiful; it is, "that which he gave her *according to the hand* of King Solomon." We may link this with David's grateful words: "*According to Thine own heart* hast Thou done all these great things"; and again: "Thou hast dealt well with Thy servant, O Lord, *according to Thy word.*" His hand, His heart, His word—what an immeasurable measure of His bounty! The great *hand* that holds the ocean in its hollow is opened to satisfy our desire, and to go beyond that exceeding abundantly, giving us according to the *heart* that "*so* loved the world," and according to the *word* which is so deep and full that all the saints that ever drew their hope and joy from it cannot fathom its ever up-springing fountain.

Perhaps nobody knows the Bible well enough to know the full significance of saying, "Be it unto me *according to Thy word,*" how much less can we imagine what shall be the yet unrevealed royal bounty *according to His heart* of infinite love and hand of infinite power! "What I do thou knowest not now, but thou shalt know hereafter." "And ye shall …

Joel 2:26 | be satisfied, and praise the name of the Lord your God, that hath dealt wondrously with you."

> When this passing world is done,
> When has sunk yon glaring sun,
> When we stand with Christ in glory,
> Looking o'er life's finished story,
> Then, Lord, shall I fully know—
> Not till then—how much I owe!
>
> R. M'Cheyne.

SECOND DAY.

The Opened Treasure.

"The Lord shall open unto thee His good treasure."—Deuteronomy 28:12.

Matthew 2:11	WHEN the wise men "opened their treasures," they brought out gold and frankincense and myrrh. When Jehovah opens unto us His good treasure, we shall see greater things than these.
John 1:50	
	The context of this rich promise seems to make "the heaven" the treasure-house; and in its primary and literal sense, the fertilizing rain is the first outpouring of the opened treasure, soon after expanded into beautiful details
Deut. 33:13–16	of the "precious things of heaven and … the precious things of the earth." But the spiritual blessings are closely interwoven with the temporal in the whole passage, and the faithful Israelites who did not "look only for transitory promises" may well have claimed the opening of heavenly treasure through this promise.
Deut. 28:1–14	
Article 7 [of the 39 Articles of the Church of England]	
Ephesians 3:8	What shall He "open unto thee"? In a word, "the unsearchable riches of Christ." In Him "are hid all the treasures of wisdom and knowledge," but the Lord shall open them unto thee. Riches of goodness, and forbearance, and long-suffering shall be meted out in infinitely gracious proportion to our sins, and provocations, and repeated waywardness; exceeding riches of grace for all our poverty now, and riches in glory enough and to spare for all the needs of glorified capacities through all eternity. "All are yours" in Him.
Colossians 2:3	
Romans 2:4	
Ephesians 2:7	
Philippians 4:19	
1 Cor. 3:22	
Ephesians 2:8	Faith is the key to this infinite treasury, and in giving us faith He gives us treasure for treasure. He is ready to make us "rich in faith," and then still to "increase our faith" "unto all riches of the full assurance of understanding." Ask
James 2:5; Lk 17:5	
Colossians 2:2	

for this golden key, and then put it into the Lord's hand, that He may turn it in the lock.

He shall open unto thee the good treasure not only of the living Word, but of the written word. This is indeed "treasure to be desired," "more to be desired than gold"; and when Jehovah the Spirit opens this to us, we shall, we *do*, rejoice "as one that findeth great spoil." Christ, the true Wisdom, has said, "I will fill their treasures," and "the chambers shall be filled with all precious and pleasant riches." So that when He has done this we are "made treasurers over treasuries," and may "bring forth out of" our "treasure things new and old."

It is only with God-given treasure that we can enrich others. When we want to give a word to another, it generally seems to come with more power if, instead of casting about for what we think likely to suit them, we simply hand over to them any treasure word which He has freshly given to ourselves. When He opens to us some shining bit of treasure, let us not forget: "Freely ye have received, freely *give*."

Also, let us not stand idly waiting for some further opening of the treasure, but "let there be *search* made in the king's treasure-house," "in the house of the rolls where the treasures were laid up," where the "decrees" and "records" of our King are to be "found." They are truly "hidden riches." Neither must we trust in our own store of spiritual treasures, whether of memory, experience, or even of grace, or we shall soon come under the condemning word, "O backsliding daughter, that trusted in her treasures!" No, it is only continual drawing from *His* good treasure that will profit us, even "the light of the knowledge of the glory of God in the face of Jesus Christ." And "we have *this* treasure in earthen vessels, that the excellency of the power may be of God and not of us."

Margin references:

Luke 24:32
Prov 21:20; Psalm 19:10
Psalm 119:162
Proverbs 8:21
Proverbs 24:4
Nehemiah 13:13
Matthew 13:52

Matthew 10:8

Proverbs 2:4
Ezra 5:17
Ezra 6:1
Ezra 6:2
Isaiah 45:3
Jeremiah 48:7

Jeremiah 49:4

2 Cor. 4:6
2 Cor. 4:7

THIRD DAY.

The King's Signature and Seal.

"The writing which is written in the king's name, and sealed with the king's ring, may no man reverse."—Esther 8:8.

<table>
<tr><td>

2 Peter 1:4
Psalm 119:97
2 Peter 1:17–19

John 1:1
John 17:4, 6, 26

John 17:14

Ephesians 1:13,
etc.

John 12:48
2 Samuel 23:2

Mark 12:36;
1 Peter 1:11
1 Thess. 2:13

Hebrews 4:12
Daniel 6:17

</td><td>

SUCH is the writing which by God's great goodness is the glory of our land and the treasure of our hearts, full of exceeding great and precious promises, of commands not less great and not less precious, and of words of prophecy (which are only words of promise a little farther off) "more sure" than the testimony of an apostle's senses to the excellent glory and the heavenly voice.

It is written in the King's name. The living Word of God, who came to declare, to manifest, and to glorify the Father, has imprinted His own name upon the same testimony as written by the Spirit, and has given it to us as the "word of God."

It is sealed with the King's ring. Sealing is a special work of the Holy Spirit, exercised in different ways; and how clearly has he sealed this great writing with the King's ring, engraved with His own image and superscription, the convincing token of its being indeed from Himself, and sent forth in unchangeable authority and power!

It is a double sealing, without and within—first, the external and distinctly visible declaration that the writing is "by the Holy Ghost"; and then the all-convincing evidence that it is so by its effectual working in our own hearts with a power which, we know for ourselves, cannot be less than almighty and therefore divine.

It is thus written in the King's name, and "sealed with His own signet," not only that we may know it to be His, but that we may have the right humbly, yet confidently, to show Him, so to speak, His own name and His own signet

</td></tr>
</table>

as our claim for the fulfilment of all contained therein. He will never fail to acknowledge them.

This royal writing "may no man reverse." The King Himself cannot reverse it, for He changes not; He "*cannot lie,*" "He *cannot* deny Himself:" for unchangeable truth is not only an essential attribute, but the very essence of His Deity. This one great "cannot" is the security for all that He "can" and will do.

And if God "cannot," who can? All "the craft and subtilty" of devil or man is powerless against one syllable of this royal writing. "The word of our God shall stand for ever," and the hoarse recoil of every furious wave that is shattered into foam against this everlasting rock only murmurs, "I *cannot* reverse it."

And is it not a most blessed and comforting thought that we ourselves cannot reverse it, though this is the quarter from which we are practically most tempted to dread its reversal? For, "if we believe not, yet He abideth faithful." All the earth-born or devil-breathed fogs and clouds of doubt, from the fall till this hour, have not been able to touch the splendour of one star that He has set in the unassailable firmament of His eternal truth.

All the promises of God are yea and Amen—where?—"*in Him,*" the Son of God. He holds these stars in His right hand; He has held the great promise of eternal life for us since God gave it to Him for us before the world began, and every other is subincluded. And it is one of His offices "to confirm the promises." Signed, sealed, held, and confirmed thus, should not "It is written" be enough for our present "light, and gladness, and joy, and honour"?

Another clause of this beautiful verse is too striking to be passed over: "Write ye also for the Jews, *as it liketh you,* in the king's name, and seal it with the king's ring." Does not this remind us of another writing of our King: "If ye abide in me, and my words abide in you, ye shall ask *what ye will,* and it shall be done unto you." He places His own name and His own signet at the disposal of His "abiding" ones, and says: "Ask Me of things to come concerning My sons, and concerning the work of My hands *command ye*

Me." "Thou shalt also decree a thing, and it shall be established unto thee." Should not this encourage us in intercession? Perhaps we are saying, like Esther, "How can I endure to see the destruction of my kindred?" Have we as yet *fully* availed ourselves of "the King's name," and "the King's ring"?

> For He hath given us a changeless writing,
>   Royal decrees that light and gladness bring,
> Signed with His name in glorious inditing,
>   Sealed on our hearts with His own signet ring.

Job 22:28

Esther 8:6

FOURTH DAY.

The Candour of Christ.

"Come, see a man which told me all things that ever I did: is not this the Christ?"
—John 4:29.

John 4:25

John 4:29

YES! it is not merely a vague general belief in Christ as the Teacher who "will tell *us* all things" which suffices for heart conviction of "the reality of Jesus Christ," but the individual knowledge of Him as the Searcher who "told *me* all things that ever I did." This was what led the woman of Samaria to exclaim, "Is not this the Christ?" this was to her the irresistible proof of His Messiahship.

What about ourselves? If we know anything of true intercourse with the Lord Jesus, our experience will not be unlike hers. When He who "searches Jerusalem with candles" turns the keen flame of His eyes upon the dark corners of our hearts, and flashes their far-reaching, all-revealing beam upon even the far-off and long-forgotten windings of our lives; when in His light we see the darkness, and in His purity we see the sin that has been, or that is; when He "declareth unto man what is his thought," and then convinces that "as he thinketh in his heart, so *is* he," *then* we know for ourselves that He "with whom we have to do" is "indeed the Christ."

Zephaniah 1:12
Rev. 2:18, 23
1 Sam. 16:7; 1 Ch. 28:9; Job 13:26; 42:5, 6; Isaiah 6:5

Amos 4:13
Proverbs 23:7
Hebrews 4:13
John 4:42

He does not merely *show* us; it is something more than that. It is not merely an invisible hand drawing away a veil from hidden scenes, and a light brought to bear upon them, so that we can see them if we will; it is more personal, more terrible, and yet more tender than that. He *tells* us what we have done; and, if we listen, the telling will be very clear, very thorough, very unmistakable.

1 Kings 19:12
2 Samuel 12:7

At first we are tempted not to listen at all; we shrink from the still small voice which tells us such startlingly unwelcome things.

Many feel what one expressed: "Whenever I *do* think about it, I feel so horribly bad that I don't like to think any more." Ah, "if thou hadst known, even thou, at least in this thy day," that it was not mere "thinking about it," but the voice of the Saviour beginning to tell thee what would have cleared the way for "the things which belong unto thy peace," what blessing might not the patient and willing listening have brought! Oh, do not stifle the voice, do not fancy it is only uncomfortable thoughts which you will not encourage lest they should make you low-spirited! Instead of that, ask Him to let His voice sound louder and clearer, and believe "that the goodness of God leadeth thee to repentance." Only listen, and He will tell you not only all things that ever *you* did, but all things which He has done for you. He never leaves off in the middle of all He has to tell, unless we wilfully interrupt Him.

Perhaps we have gone through all this, and known the humbling blessedness of being searched and "told," and then pardoned and cleansed; and now again there is something not right. We hardly know what, only there is a misgiving, a dim, vague uneasiness; we "really don't know of anything in particular," and yet there is something unsatisfied and unsatisfactory. There is nothing for it but to come to our Messiah afresh, and ask Him to tell us what we have done, or are doing, which is not in accordance with His will. It will be useless coming if we are not sincerely purposed to let Him tell us what He will, and not merely what we expect; or if we hush up the first word of an unwelcome whisper, and say, "Oh, *that* can't have anything to do with it!" or, "I am all right *there,* at any rate!" We must simply say, "Master, say on"; and perhaps He will then show us, as He did Simon, that we have not done Him the true and loving service which some poor despised one has rendered.

Oh, never shrink from the probings of our beloved Physician. Dearer and dearer will the hand become as we yield to it. Sweeter and sweeter will be the proofs that He is our own *faithful* Friend, who only wounds that He may perfectly heal.

Luke 19:42

Isaiah 48:18

Luke 7:40
Romans 2:4
Psalm 85:8
1 Samuel 12:24

Psalm 94:12
Psalm 32:1
2 Samuel 21:1
Job 15:11; 10:2

Psalm 139:23
Matthew 7:21
Job 13:22, 23

Luke 7:40

Luke 7:44–46

Matthew 9:12
Job 5:18

Proverbs 27:6

Only this I know, I tell Him all my doubts, and griefs, and fears;
Oh, how patiently He listens, and my drooping soul He cheers!
Do you think He ne'er reproves me? What a false friend He would be,
If He never, never told me of the sins which He must see!

Do you think that I could love Him half so well, or as I ought,
If He did not tell me plainly of each sinful deed and thought?
No! He is very faithful, and that makes me trust Him more;
For I know that He *does* love me, though He wounds me very sore.

Ellen Lakshmi Goreh.

FIFTH DAY.

From Death unto Life.

"Is passed from death unto life."—John 5:24.

TWO distinct states with nothing between. No broad space between the two where we may stand, leading to the one or to the other; only a boundary line too fine to balance upon. Not many steps—not even two or three from one to the other, but one step *from* death *unto* life; the foot lifted *from* the hollow crust over the volcanic fire, and set *upon* the Rock of salvation.

Acts 26:18

Psalm 40:2

How tremendously important to know whether this step is taken; but how clear and simple the test: "He that heareth My word, and believeth on Him that sent Me, hath everlasting life, and shall not come into condemnation; but is passed from death unto life." Are you trembling and down-hearted, wanting some very strong consolation for your very weak faith? Lay hold of this. See how the rope is let down low enough to meet the hand which you can scarcely lift.

Hebrews 6:18
1 Timothy 6:12
Hebrews 12:12

"He that heareth My word." Can you say you have *not* heard? You have heard His word *as* His word, recognising it as such, receiving it "not as the word of men, but as it is in truth, the word of God." It "is come unto you," because it "is sent" unto you. The word of Jesus is heard by your innermost self, and you would not be hearing and recognising it if you were still dead. A marble statue hears not.

1 Thess. 2:13
Colossians 1:6

"And believeth on Him that sent Me." "But that is the very question," you say; "if I were sure I believed, I should know I had everlasting life." Why should you know? Because He says so, and you could not but believe what He says. Then listen now to what He says: "The Father sent the Son to be the Saviour of the world." Do you *not* be-

John 6:47
1 John 4:14

John 3:16 John 16:9	lieve this? Did the Father *not* send the Son? Did He *not* so love the world? Let the very recoil from such plain English of unbelief show you the sin and folly of doubting any more. You do hear His word, you do believe on the Father who sent the Son to be your Saviour, will you not now be-
John 5:24	lieve that Jesus means what He says in threefold assurance: "Hath everlasting life, and shall not come into condemnation; but is passed from death unto life"?
	Not "is passing," but "is passed"; a fact whose full blessedness cannot be fully realized here, while we only "know
1 Cor. 13:12 Rom. 6:23; 2 Tim. 2:13	in part" God's great gift of eternal life, but not affected by varying degrees of realization.
	See your position,—or rather, take His word about it,—and give Him thanks—oh, give Him thanks—for having lifted you in your blindness and helplessness over that solemn boundary line when you could not even step over it.
Isaiah 44:23 2 Chron. 20:22	"Sing ... for the Lord hath done it"; and when you begin to sing and to praise, the Lord's own ambushments of promises will start up before your eyes (*there* all the time, only you did not see them), and the shadowy hosts of fears and doubts
1 John 3:14	shall flee away, and you shall "*know*" that you have passed from death unto life.
	From death—cold, dark, hopeless, useless, loveless; the
Ephesians 2:1 Revelation 20:14 John 10:10 Ps. 23:4; Jn. 11:26	death in trespasses and sins; the death that lives (strange paradox) for ever in the lake of fire—unto life with its ever-increasing abundance; life crowned with light and love; life upon which only a shadow of death can ever pass, and that only the shadow of the portal of eternal glory; life in Jesus,
1 Thess. 5:10	life for Jesus, life with Jesus.
Ephesians 2:13 Colossians 1:21 Luke 15:32; Eph. 2:19; 5:8	This is your position now—made nigh instead of far off; reconciled to God instead of "enemies in your mind"; found instead of lost; fellow-citizens with the saints instead of strangers and foreigners; sometimes darkness, but now light in the Lord; passed from death unto life. And all be-
Philippians 2:8	cause Jesus passed from life unto death, even the death of the cross, for you; because it was the Father's will that He
Psalm 40:9, P.B.V. Psalm 40:10	should come as the only required "sacrifice for sin"; and He, our Lord Jesus Christ, was "content to do it."

There is life for a look at the Crucified One;
    There is life at this moment for thee;
Then look, sinner—look unto Him, and be saved—
    Unto Him who was nailed to the tree.

Oh, doubt not thy welcome, since God has declared
    There remaineth no more to be done;
That once in the end of the world He appeared,
    And completed the work He begun.

But take, with rejoicing, from Jesus at once
    The life everlasting He gives:
And know, with assurance, thou never canst die,
    Since Jesus, thy Righteousness, lives.

A. M. Hull.

SIXTH DAY.

Justified.

"And by Him all that believe are justified from all things, from which ye could not be justified by the law of Moses."—Acts 13:39.

Isaiah 61:10	"**And.**" For justification does not come first. The robe of righteousness is not put on until the sinner is "purged from his old sins." So this is God's order—first, "Through this man is preached unto you the forgiveness of sins"; and then, "By Him all that believed are justified."
2 Peter 1:9	
Psalm 143:2	But "in Thy sight shall no man living be justified." "For not the hearers of the law are just before God, but the doers of the law shall be justified." But we have *not* "obeyed the voice of the Lord our God, to walk in His laws, which He set before us." So "that no man is justified by the law in the sight of God, it is evident"; for "by the deeds of the law there shall no flesh be justified in His sight." "How then can man be justified with God?" "The law was our schoolmaster to bring us unto Christ, that we might be justified by faith."
Romans 2:13	
Daniel 9:10	
Galatians 3:11	
Romans 3:20	
Job 25:4	
Galatians 3:24	
Romans 3:24	This glorious justification by faith is sevenfold; We are justified, 1. "*By His grace*"—the grace of God the Father, one of whose most wonderful titles is, "The Justifier of him which believeth in Jesus." 2. "*By His blood*"—that precious blood which has to do with every stage of our redemption and effectuated salvation; from the writing of our names "in the book of life of the Lamb slain from the foundation of the world," till the chorus of the "new song" is full in heaven. 3. "*By the Righteousness of One*" (of the One), "by the obedience of One"; by which the free gift, the unspeakable gift of eternal life—nay, of Christ Himself to be our life—"came upon all men unto justification of life." 4. *By the resurrection* of Jesus our Lord, who "was raised again for
Romans 3:26	
Romans 5:9	
Revelation 13:8	
Revelation 5:9	
Romans 5:18, 19	
2 Cor. 9:15;	
Romans 6:23	
Colossians 3:4	
Romans 4:24, 25	

our justification," the grand token that our Substitute had indeed fulfilled all righteousness for us.

> "For God released our Surety
> To show the work was done."

5. "*By His knowledge* shall My righteous Servant justify many; for He shall bear their iniquities." For true faith is founded upon the knowledge of Him, and "this is life eternal." 6. *By faith*; just *only* believing God's word; and accepting God's way about it. 7. *By works*; because these are the necessary and inseparable evidence that faith is not mere fancy or talk. We *are* "justified by faith without the deeds of the law," the old dead galvanic struggle to do duties and keep outward obligations; but *not* without works, which "do spring out necessarily from a true and lively faith"; for "faith without works is *dead*."

"Therefore, being justified by faith," what then? 1. "We have peace with God." 2. "We shall be saved from wrath through Him." 3. We are made heirs of eternal life. 4. We shall be glorified by Him and with Him for ever.

What about my own part and lot in the matter? Whom does God thus justify? and may I hope to be among them? He begins indeed at the lowest depth, so that none may be shut out; for He "would justify the heathen through faith," and He "justifieth the ungodly." The publican who could only cry, "God be merciful to me the sinner," was justified. I can come in here, at all events.

But how shall I be actually and effectually justified *now*? Let God speak and I will listen: "Even the righteousness of God which is by faith of Jesus Christ unto *all* and upon *all* them that believe: for there is no difference." "By Him all that believe *are* justified." "I believe in Jesus Christ His only Son our Lord." Do I? "Lord, I *believe*." Then His righteousness is upon me, and I *am* justified. "Knowing that a man is not justified by the works of the law, but by the faith of Jesus Christ, even we have believed in Jesus Christ, that we might be justified by the faith of Christ." And now, "He is *near* that justifieth me." "Who shall lay anything to the charge of God's elect? It is God that justifieth."

Justified.

Romans 3:24	By the grace of God the Father, thou art freely justified,
Romans 5:9	Through the great redemption purchased by the blood of Him who died,
Romans 10:4	By His life, for thee fulfilling God's command exceeding broad,
Romans 4:25	By His glorious resurrection, seal and signet of our God.
Romans 5:1	Therefore, justified for ever by the faith which He hath given,
Romans 15:13	Peace, and joy, and hope abounding smooth thy trial-path to heaven:
Hosea 2:19	Unto Him betrothed for ever, who thy life shall crown and bless,
Jeremiah 33:16	By His name thou shalt be called, Christ, "The Lord our Righteousness."

SEVENTH DAY.

The Royal Wine.

"Thy love is better than wine."—Song of Solomon 1:2.

Esther 1:7
John 14:27

Hosea 6:3
Ephesians 3:19
Ephesians 3:18

Revelation 7:9

Genesis 27:38
Galatians 2:20

1 John 2:17
1 Cor. 7:29–31
John 13:1
Jeremiah 31:3

Proverbs 14:13
Eccles. 2:10, 11
John 4:13

Isaiah 59:12, 13, 16

WINE is the symbol of earthly joy; and who that has had but one sip of the love of Christ does not know this "royal wine," this true "wine of the kingdom," to be better than the best joy that the world can give! How much more, then, when deeper and fuller draughts are the daily portion, as we "follow on to know" the love "which passeth knowledge"! It is the privilege not of a favoured few, but of "*all* saints," to comprehend something of what is incomprehensible.

1. The breadth, contrasted with the narrowness of earthly love and all its joy. Perhaps it is not so much by looking at His love to all the redeemed ones whom no man can number, that we realize this, as by seeing that the love of Jesus was broad enough to reach and include "even me." "Who loved *me*"; is not that more incomprehensible than that He loved all the saints and angels?

2. The length, contrasted with the passing shortness of the longest earthly love and joy. What is the length? "Unto the end." And even that is not the full measure, for His immeasurable love is everlasting; and when inconceivable ages have passed, we shall be no nearer "the end" than now.

3. The depth, contrasted with the shallowness which is always felt, however disguised, in the world's best. Down to the very depth of our fall went that wonderful love of Christ, to the depth of our sin, to the depth of our need, to the depth of those caverns of our own strange inner being which we ourselves cannot fathom, and which only His love can fill.

4. The height, contrasted with the lowness and littleness of all that is represented by the world's wine. This all ends in self, which is like a low vaulted roof, keeping down every possibility of rising; and so the earthly joy can take but a bat-like flight, always checked, always limited, in dusk and darkness. But the love of Christ breaks through the vaulting, and leads us up into the free sky above, expanding to the very throne of Jehovah, and drawing us "still upward" to the infinite heights of glory. Is there any height beyond, "*As* the Father hath loved Me, *so* have I loved *you*"? These measures (so to speak) of Christ's love are those of the unsearchable perfection of God Himself! "It is as high as heaven, deeper than hell" (thank God for that word deeper), "longer than the earth, and broader than the sea."

For whom is this love? Oh how glad we are that it is not for the worthy and the faithful, so that we must be shut out, but for His own, *though* the chief of sinners! It is "the love of the Lord toward the children of Israel, who look to other gods, and love flagons of wine." Has it been so with us, that we have been looking away from Jesus to heart-idols and "other lords," and loving some earthly "flagons of wine"—other love, other pleasures, other joys, "other things," which are *not* Jesus Christ's? Then only think of "the love of the Lord toward" *us!* Well may we say, "Thy love to me was wonderful," and own it to be "better than wine," "above my chief joy." He proved His love to you and me to be "strong as death"; and when all God's waves and billows went over Him, the many waters could not quench it.

In His love and in His pity He redeemed us; in the same love He bears us and carries us all the day long. He "loveth at *all* times," and that includes this present moment; now, while your eye is on this page, His eye of love is looking on you, and the folds of His banner of love are overshadowing you.

Is there even a feeble pulse of love to Him? He meets it with, "I love them that love Me." "I will love him, and will manifest Myself to him." And so surely as the bride says, "Thy love is better than wine," so surely does the heavenly Bridegroom respond with incomprehensible condescension:

Margin references:
Ps. 139:6; Eccles. 1:14; 2:17, 18
Isaiah 2:6

Ezekiel 41:7

John 15:9

Job 11:7–9

John 13:1; 1 Tim. 1:15; Hosea 3:1

Isaiah 26:13
Mark 4:19
Philippians 2:21
2 Samuel 1:26
Psalm 137:6
Song. 8:6
Psalm 42:7
Song. 8:7
Isaiah 63:9
Isaiah 46:4
Proverbs 17:17

Song. 2:4

Proverbs 8:17
John 14:21

Song. 4:10
2 Cor. 5:14
Galatians 2:20

"How fair is *thy* love, my sister, my spouse! how much better is *thy* love than wine." May this love of Christ constrain us to live unto Him "who loved me and gave Himself for me."

> O Christ, He is the fountain,
>   The deep, sweet well of love!
> The streams on earth I've tasted,
>   More deep I'll drink above.
> There to an ocean-fulness
>   His mercy doth expand,
> Where glory, glory dwelleth
>   In Immanuel's land.
>
> Oh! I am my Beloved's,
>   And my Beloved is mine!
> He brings a poor vile sinner
>   Into His "house of wine."
> I stand upon His merits;
>   I know no safer stand,
> Not e'en where glory dwelleth
>   In Immanuel's land.

A. R. Cousin.

EIGHTH DAY.

The Gift of Peace.

"My peace I give unto you."—John 14:27.

"PEACE I leave with you" is much; "My peace I give unto you" is more. The added word tells the fathomless marvel of the gift—"My peace." Not merely "peace with God"; Christ has made that by the blood of His cross, and being justified by faith we have it through Him. But after we are thus reconciled, the enmity and the separation being ended, Jesus has a gift for us from His own treasures; and this is its special and wonderful value, that it is *His very own*. How we value a gift which was the giver's own possession! what a special token of intimate friendship we feel it to be! To others we give what we have made or purchased; it is only to very near and dear ones that we give what has been our own personal enjoyment or use. And so Jesus gives us not only peace made and peace purchased, but a share in His very own peace,—divine, eternal, incomprehensible peace,—which dwells in His own heart as God, and which shone in splendour of calmness through His life as man. No wonder that it "passeth all understanding."

But how? Why does the sap flow from the vine to the branch? Simply because the branch is joined to the vine. Then the sap flows into it by the very law of its nature. So, being joined to our Lord Jesus by faith, that which is His becomes ours, and flows into us by the very law of our spiritual life. If there were no hindrance, it would indeed flow as a river. Then how earnestly we should seek to have every barrier removed to the inflowing of such a gift! Let it be our prayer that He would clear the way for it, that He would take away all the unbelief, all the self, all the hidden cloggings of the channel.

Side references:
Colossians 1:20
Romans 5:1
Eph. 2:15, 16
Psalm 68:18

Proverbs 17:8

John 17:22

Philippians 4:7
John 15:5
1 Cor. 6:17
John 1:16
Ephesians 3:19
Psalm 133:2
Isaiah 48:18

Margin references:
John 15:10, 11

2 Cor. 12:9; Isaiah 11:10, mar.; Heb. 4:5; Jn. 17:22, 24
1 Thess. 4:17

Then He will give a sevenfold blessing: "My peace," "My joy," "My love," at once and always, now and for ever; "My grace" and "My strength" for all the needs of our pilgrimage; "My rest" and "My glory" for all the grand sweet home-life of eternity with Him.

> Thy reign is perfect peace,
>   Not mine, but Thine;
> A stream that cannot cease,
> For its fountain is Thy heart. Oh, depth unknown!
> Thou givest of Thine own,
>   Pouring from Thine, and filling mine.

NINTH DAY.

The Abiding Joy.

"These things have I spoken unto you, that My joy might remain in you; and that your joy might be full."—John 15:11.

Job 5:1, 8
1 Kings 22:5
Job 16:2
Ezekiel 13:22

Isaiah 8:20

Isaiah 7:9

John 15:11

John 16:24
John 17:13

1 John 1:4
1 John 2:27

WHO that has known anything of joy in the Lord but has asked, "But will it last?" And why has the question been so often the very beginning of its not lasting? Because we have either asked it of ourselves or of others, and not of the Lord only. His own answers to this continually recurring question are so different from the cautious, chilling, saddening ones which His children so often give. They are absolute, full, reiterated. We little realize how unscriptural we are when we meet His good gift of joy to ourselves or to others with a doubtful, and therefore faithless, "*If* it lasts!"

"To the law and to the testimony," O happy Christian! there you shall find true and abundant answer to your only shadow on the brightness of the joy. So long as you believe your Lord's word about it, so long it *will* last. So soon as you ask of other counsellors, and believe their word instead, so soon it will fail. Jesus meets your difficulty explicitly. He has provided against it by giving the very reason why He spoke the gracious words of His last discourse, "That My joy might *remain* in you." Is not this exactly what we were afraid to hope, what seemed too good to be true, that it "might *remain*"? And lest we should think that this abiding joy only meant some moderate measure of qualified joy, He adds, "And that your joy may be *full*," repeating in the next chapter, and intensifying it in the next. And lest we might think this was said with reference only to an exceptional case, He inspired His beloved disciple to echo the words in his *general* epistle: "That your joy may be full," and "the anointing which ye have received of Him abideth in you."

Never in His word are we told anything contradicting or explaining away this precious and reiterated promise. All through we are brightly pointed not merely to hope of permanence, but to increase. "The meek shall increase (not merely shall keep up) their joy in the Lord." There are mingled promises and commands as to growth and increase in grace, knowledge, love, strength, and peace, and does not increase of these imply and ensure joy? Is joy to be the *only* fruit of the Spirit of which it may not be said that it " sprang up and *increased*"?

When it is suggested that we "cannot" (some even say, "must not") "expect to be always joyful," remember that "it is written," "Rejoice in the Lord" (not "sometimes," but) "*alway*." "As sorrowful, yet *alway* rejoicing." When we are told that "it would not even be good for us," remember that "it is written again," "The joy of the Lord is your strength." Perhaps in that word "of" lies the whole secret of lasting joy; for it is more than even "joy *in* the Lord:" it is His own joy flowing into the soul that is joined to Himself, which alone can "remain" in us, not even our joy in Him. "That they might have *My* joy fulfilled in themselves." Let us, then, seek not the stream, but the fountain; not primarily the joy, but that real and living union with Jesus by which His joy becomes ours.

Let us not, either for ourselves or others, acquiesce in disobedience to any of His commandments. See how absolute they are! "Serve the Lord with gladness"; "Rejoice in the Lord, ye righteous," and many others. Turn to the terribly distinct condemnation, "Because thou servedst not the Lord thy God with joyfulness, and with gladness of heart, ... therefore shalt thou serve thine enemies, ... and He shall put a yoke of iron on thy neck until He have destroyed thee."

No one need be cast down because they cannot *yet* tell of abiding joy, or because others cannot tell of it. Thank God, our experience is not the measure of His promises; they are all yea and Amen in Christ Jesus, and our varying, short-falling experience touches neither their faithfulness nor their fulness. Forget the things which are behind, and press on to firmer grasp and fuller reception of Christ and His joy. Then it shall be always "praise ... more and more," "more grace," "grace for grace," "from strength to strength,"—yes, even "from glory to glory." Then you shall indeed "hold fast the confidence and the *rejoicing* of the hope firm unto the end."

May I earnestly ask every reader who is saying, "Will it last?" to seek "out of the book of the Lord" for themselves; taking a concordance, and looking out, under the words, Joy, Rejoice, Gladness, etc., the overwhelming reiterations of promises and commands which can leave them in no doubt as to God's answer.

Ps. 71:14; James 4:6; John 1:16
Ps. 84:7; 2 Cor. 3:18; Heb. 3:6

Isaiah 34:16

Psalm 85:8

TENTH DAY.

The Sure Afterward.

"Now no chastening for the present seemeth to be joyous, but grievous: nevertheless, afterward it yieldeth the peaceable fruit of righteousness unto them which are exercised thereby."—Hebrews 12:11.

<small>Exodus 3:7
Deut. 8:5
Hebrews 12:5

Prov. 3:11; Psalm 94:12; 2 Cor. 4:17; 1 Peter 1:7
Hebrews 12:6</small>

THERE are some promises which we are apt to reserve for great occasions, and thus lose the continual comfort of them. Perhaps we read this one with a sigh, and say: "How beautiful this is for those whom the Lord is really chastening! I almost think I should not mind that, if such a promise might then be mine. But the things that try me are only little things that turn up every day to trouble and depress me." Well, now, does the Lord specify what degree of trouble, or what kind of trouble, is great enough to make up a claim to the promise? And if He does not, why should you? He only defines it as "not joyous, but grievous." Perhaps there have been a dozen different things to-day which were "not joyous, but grievous" to you. And though you feel ashamed of feeling them so much, and hardly like to own to their having been so trying, and would not think of dignifying them as "chastening," yet, if they come under the Lord's definition, He not only knows all about them, but they were, every one of them, chastenings from His hand; neither to be despised and called "just nothing" when all the while they *did* "grieve" you; nor to be wearied of; because they are working out blessing to you and glory to Him. Every one of them has been an unrecognised token of His love and interest in you; for "whom the Lord loveth He chasteneth."

Next, do not let us reserve this promise for chastenings in the aggregate. Notice the singular pronoun, "Nevertheless, afterward IT yieldeth," not "*they* yield." Does not this

The Sure Afterward.

indicate that every separate chastening has its own especial "afterward"? We think of trials as intended to do us good in the long-run, and in a general sort of way; but the Lord says of each one, "*It* yieldeth." Apply this to "the present." The particular annoyance which befell you this morning; the vexatious words which met your ear and "grieved" your spirit; the disappointment which was His appointment for to-day; the slight but hindering ailment; the presence of some one who is "a grief of mind" to you; whatever this day seemeth not joyous, but grievous, is linked in "the good pleasure of His goodness," with a corresponding afterward of "peaceable fruit"; the very seed from which, if you only do not choke it, this shall spring and ripen.

If we set ourselves to watch the Lord's dealings with us, we shall often be able to detect a most beautiful correspondence and proportion between each individual "chastening" and its own resulting "afterward." The habit of thus watching and expecting will be very comforting, and a great help to quiet trust when some new chastening is sent: for then we shall simply consider it as the herald and earnest of a new "afterward."

Lastly, do not let us reserve this promise for some far future time. The Lord did not say "*a long while* afterward," and do not let us gratuitously insert it. It rather implies that, as soon as the chastening is over, the peaceable fruit shall appear "unto the glory and praise of God." So let us look out for the "afterward" as soon as the pressure is past. This immediate expectation will bring its own blessing if we can say, "My expectation is from Him," and not from any fruit-bearing qualities of our own; for only "from Me is thy fruit found." Fruit from Him will also be fruit unto Him.

Romans 8:28

Genesis 31:12
Psalm 69:26

Genesis 26:35
2 Thess. 1:11

Psalm 90:15
Micah 7:15
Job 42:11, 12

Philippians 1:11

Psalm 62:5
Hosea 14:8
Romans 7:4

> What shall Thine afterward be, O Lord?
> I wonder, and wait to see
> (While to Thy chastening hand I bow)
> What peaceable fruit may be ripening now,
> Ripening fast for Thee!

ELEVENTH DAY.

No Hurt.

"Nothing shall by any means hurt you."—Luke 10:19.

IS not this one of those very strong promises which we are apt to think are worded a little *too* strongly, and off which we "take a great discount"? Now, instead of daring a "Yea, hath God said?" let us just take *all* the comfort and rest and gladness of it for ourselves. Let us believe every word, just as our beloved Master uttered it to the simple-hearted seventy who were so surprised to find His name so much more powerful than they expected.

Nothing! If He said "nothing," have we any right to add, "Yes, but *except* ... "? Nothing can hurt those who are joined to Christ, for "with me thou shalt be in safeguard," unless anything could be found which should separate us from Him. And "who shall separate us?" Earthly tribulations, even the most terrible, shall not do it, for "in all these things we are more than conquerors through Him that loved us." Yet a farther reaching and, indeed, entirely exhaustive list is given, none of which, " nor *any* other creature, shall be able to separate us." Let us take everything that possibly could hurt us to that list, and see for ourselves if it is not included, and then rejoice in the conclusion, based and built upon Christ's bare word, but buttressed and battlemented by this splendid utterance of His inspired apostle that it is indeed so—"*nothing* shall by any means hurt you."

But He who knows our little faith never gives an isolated promise. He leaves us no chance of overlooking or misunderstanding any one, except by wilful neglect, because it is always confirmed in other parts of His word. So He has given the same strong consolation in other terms. "The Lord shall preserve thee from *all* evil" (do you believe *that*?).

Margin references:
Genesis 3:1
Proverbs 30:5
Luke 10:17

1 Samuel 22:23

Romans 8:35
Romans 8:37

Romans 8:38, 39

Matthew 8:26

Hebrews 6:18
Psalm 121:7

No Hurt.   29

Proverbs 12:21
Job 5:19; Ps 91:10

Daniel 3:25
Daniel 6:22, 23
Acts 18:10

Ps. 146:6, P.B.V.
Zechariah 2:5
Psalm 91:7
Zechariah 2:8
Psalm 17:7,8
Luke 10:16
Isaiah 63:1
1 Peter 3:13

Isaiah 54:17; Ps. 31:20; Deut. 23:5
Isaiah 27:3

Eccles. 8:5

Romans 8:28
Phil. 1:12, 19;
2 Cor. 4:17; Isa. 38:16; cf. Genesis 42:36; 45:5–13

Psalm 119:42

John 20:28
Psalm 4:8

"There shall *no* evil happen to the just." "In seven (troubles) there shall no evil touch thee." Then see how He individualized it to Shadrach, Meshach, and Abednego, even *in* the burning fiery furnace, "They have no hurt"; to Daniel among the lions, "They have not hurt me"; to St. Paul among turbulent men with a care-nought governor, "No man shall set on thee to hurt thee." We are not likely to be more exposed to "hurt" than these, and we have the same God, "who keepeth His promise for ever." He is the "wall of fire round about" us; and what fortification so impenetrable—nay, so unapproachable! And "He that toucheth you toucheth the apple of His eye"—the very least touch is felt by the Lord, who loves us and is mighty to save! Well may He say, "And who is he that will harm you?"

"Nothing shall by *any* means hurt you," for "no weapon that is formed against thee shall prosper"; man's curse shall be turned into God's blessing. Jehovah Himself, watering His vineyard every moment, says: "Lest any hurt it, I will keep it night and day." Again, the promise, with a solemn condition, takes an even stronger form: "Whoso keepeth the commandment shall *feel* no evil thing."

Is not all this enough? It might well be, but His wonderful love has yet more to say—not only that nothing shall hurt us, but that all things work together for our good; not merely *shall* work, but actually *are* working. All things, if it *means* all things, must include exactly those very things, whatever they may be, which you and I are tempted to think will hurt us, or, at least, *may* hurt us. Now will we this evening trust our own ideas, or Christ's word? One or other must be mistaken. Which is it? Christ, my own Master, my Lord and my God, has given a promise which meets every fear; therefore "I will both lay me down in peace, and sleep: for Thou, Lord, only makest me to dwell in safety," and "nothing shall by any means hurt" me.

TWELFTH DAY.

The Putting Forth of the Sheep.

"When He putteth forth His own sheep, He goeth before them."—John 10:4.

Joshua 3:4

Isaiah 42:16
Isaiah 45:2
John 10:26,27;
10:3; Genesis
28:7, 15
John 10:5
Genesis 13:10

Hebrews 11:8
Gen. 28:2; 31:30
Deut. 32:11

Psalm 120:5
Genesis 39:1–2
Esther 2:16
Ruth 1:7

Isa 42:16; Jn 14:2
Psalm 139:8–10
Deut. 1:33
Hebrews 13:14

Micah 2:10
Exodus 33:14
Jeremiah 31:2
Genesis 46:3, 4

WHAT gives the Alpine climber confidence in wild, lonely, difficult passes or ascents, when he has "not passed this way heretofore"? It is that his guide has been there before; and also that in every present step over unknown and possibly treacherous ice or snow, his guide "goeth before."

It is to Christ's "own sheep" that this promise applies; simply those who believe and hear His voice. It is when *He* putteth them forth that it comes true; not when they put themselves forth, or when they let a "stranger" lure them forth, or such traitors as self-cowardice or impatience drive them forth.

Sometimes it is a literal putting forth. We have been in a sheltered nook of the fold, and we are sent to live where it is windier and wilder. The home nest is stirred up, and we have to go (it may be only for a few days, it may be for years, it may be for the rest of our lives) into less congenial surroundings, to live with fresh people, or in a different position, or in a new neighbourhood. We do not put ourselves forth, we would rather stay; but it has to be. But Jesus "goeth before." He prepares the earthly as well as the heavenly places for us. He will be there when we get to the new place. He went in the way before to search us out a place to pitch our tents in (and perhaps we were forgetting that they were tents and not palaces). If we wilfully persisted in staying where we were when He said, "Arise and depart, for this is not your rest," we should find that Presence was gone which only could cause us to rest. He is not *sending* us forth away from Him, but only *putting* us forth with

The Putting Forth of the Sheep.

Song. 2:10 Song. 4:8	His own gentle hand, saying, "Rise up, My love, and come away," "Come with Me."
	Sometimes it is putting forth into service. We had such
Song. 7:12	a nice little quiet shady corner in the vineyard, down among
Song. 1:6	the tender grapes, with such easy little weedings and water-
1 Samuel 15:17	ings to attend to. And then the Master comes and draws us
Matthew 4:19	out into the thick of the work, and puts us into a part of the
Judges 6:11, 14	field where we never should have thought of going, and puts
Exodus 3:10, 12	larger tools into our hands, that we may do more at a stroke.
Psalm 78:70, 71	And we know we are not sufficient for these things, and the
2 Cor. 2:16	very tools seem too heavy for us, and the glare too dazzling,
Jeremiah 1:6	and the vines too tall. Ah! but would we really go back? He
	would not be in the old shady corner with us now; for when
John 12:26	He put us forth He went before us, and it is only by close
John 15:5	following that we can abide with Him. Without Him we
	could do nothing if we perversely and fearfully ran back to
Philippians 4:13	our old work. With him, "through Christ which strength-
Psalm 71:16	eneth" us, we "can do all things" in the new work. Not our
Zechariah 4:6	power, but His presence will carry us through.
	Sometimes it is putting forth into the rough places of suffering, whether from temptation, pain, "or any adversity." Not one step here but Jesus has gone before us; and He still goeth before us, often so very close before us, that even
Psalm 23:2	by the still waters we never seemed so near Him. "He Him-
Heb. 2:18; 4:15	self hath suffered, being tempted." How strangely comforting to remember that He has passed even *that* way before
Hebrews 5:8	us! "The things which *He* suffered" include and cover, and
Romans 8:18	stretch wide on every side beyond, all possible "sufferings of this present time." It is in patient suffering, rather than
1 Peter 2:21	in doing, that we are specially called "to follow His steps."
Psalm 89:51, 50	"The footsteps of Thine anointed" have lain through re-
1 Peter 4:14	proach, and "the reproach of Thy servants" is no light part
Philippians 3:10	of "the fellowship of His sufferings." How specially tender
1 Peter 4:13	the Master's hand is when it is laid upon us to put us forth
Psalm 32:4	into *any* path of suffering! How specially precious, then, to
Lament. 3:31, 32	know that it is indeed His own doing!
1 Samuel 3:18	
Isaiah 38:15	
2 Cor. 6:17; Lev.	Sooner or later, perhaps again and again, He puts forth
20:26; Psalm 4:3	His own sheep into a position of greater separation—forth
2 Chron. 29:31	from an outer into an inner circle, always nearer and nearer

to the great Centre. Let us watch very sensitively for such leading. Every hesitation to yield to His gentle separation from the world results in heart separation from Him. When He thus goeth before, shall we risk being left behind?

He will put forth His own sheep at last into the path which none of them shall ever tread alone, because He trod it alone. "Yea, though I walk through the valley of the shadow of death, I will fear no evil: for Thou art with me." Our "Joshua, he shall go over before thee, as the Lord hath said." Jesus knows every single step of that valley; and when His people enter it, they will surely find that "their King shall pass before them"; and the Comforter will say, "He it is that doth go before thee."

Rev. 14:4; Luke 17:32; Hos. 4:17; 7:8; Song. 5:6

Joshua 3:11
Matthew 27:46
Psalm 23:4
Deut. 31:3
Hebrews 6:20
Micah 2:13
Deut. 31:8

THIRTEENTH DAY.

Safe Stepping.

"Thy foot shall not stumble."—Proverbs 3:23.

MANY a Christian says: "I shall be kept from falling at last; but, of course, I shall stumble continually by the way." But "have ye not read this Scripture," "Thy foot shall *not* stumble"? And if we have only once read it, ought not the "of course" to be put over on the other side? for "hath He spoken, and shall He not make it good?" "And the Scripture *cannot* be broken."

"But as a matter of fact we do stumble, and though he riseth up again, yet even the just man falleth seven times." Of course we do; and this is entirely accounted for by the other "of course." God gives us a promise, and, instead of humbly saying, "Be it unto me according to Thy word," we either altogether overlook or deliberately refuse to believe it; and then, "of course," we get no fulfilment of it. The measure of the promise is God's faithfulness; the measure of its realization is our faith. Perhaps we have not even cried, "Help Thou mine unbelief" as to this promise, much less said, "Lord, I believe."

It does not stand alone; it is reiterated and varied. He knew our constant, momentary need of it. He knew that without it we *must* stumble, and fall too; that we have not the least power to take one step without a stumble—or, rather, that we have no power to take one single onward step at all. And He knew that Satan's surest device to make us stumble would be to make us believe that "it can't be helped." We have thought that, if we have not said it.

But "what saith the Scripture?" "When thou runnest" (the likeliest pace for a slip), "thou shalt not stumble." "He will not suffer thy foot to be moved." "He will keep the feet

---

Mark 12:10

Numbers 23:19
John 10:35
Proverbs 24:16

Luke 1:38

Mark 9:24

Isaiah 7:9

Romans 4:3
Proverbs 4:12
Psalm 121:3
1 Samuel 2:9

of His saints?" He led them ... that they should not stumble." *Can* we say, "Yea, hath God said?" to all this? Leave that to Satan; it is no comment for God's children to make upon His precious promises. If we do not use the power of faith, we find the neutralizing power of unbelief.

"But how *can* I keep from stumbling?" You cannot keep from stumbling at all; but He is "able to keep you from falling," which in the Greek is strongly and distinctly "without *stumbling*." The least confidence in, or expectation from, yourself not only leads to inevitable stumbling, but is itself a grievous fall. But again we are met with the very promise we need to escape this snare: "For the Lord shall be thy confidence, and shall keep thy foot from being taken."

"Still, *how* shall I be kept?" Jesus Himself has answered: "If any man walk in the day, he stumbleth *not*, because he seeth the light of this world." "Walk in the light," "looking unto Jesus," and so shall we be "kept by the power of God through faith."

We tell a little child to look where it steps and pick its way; but Christ's little children are to do just the opposite: they are to look away to Him. "Let thine eyes look," not down, but "right on, and let thine eyelids look straight before thee." Why? Because "He it is that doth go before thee," and it is on Him, the Light of the world, that the gaze must be fixed.

"Having therefore these promises, dearly beloved," let us use them. Let us turn them into prayers of faith. "Hold up my goings in Thy paths, that my footsteps slip *not*" (did David add the whisper, "But nevertheless, of course, they *will* slip"?). "Hold Thou me up, and I *shall* be safe." "When I said, My foot slippeth; Thy mercy, O Lord, *held* me up" (not "*picked* me up').

Then comes the New Testament echo: "Yea, he shall be holden up: for God is able to make him stand." But take "all the counsel of God"; for this, too, is needed: "And thou standest by faith. Be not high-minded, but fear."

Now, if these promises are worth the paper they are written on, ought we not to believe and accept and give thanks for them, and go on our way rejoicing, claiming His prom-

---

Isaiah 63:13
Genesis 3:1

Cf. Lk 9:1, 40, and Matt 17:19, 20

Jude 24

Philippians 3:3
Jeremiah 17:5

Proverbs 3:26

John 11:9
1 John 1:7
Hebrews 12:2
1 Peter 1:5

Isaiah 45:22
Proverbs 4:25
Deut. 31:8
John 8:12

2 Cor. 7:1
Psalm 17:5

Psalm 119:117
Psalm 94:18

Romans 14:4

Acts 20:27
Romans 11:20

John 4:50

ise not once for all, not for tomorrow, but always for the *next* step of the way? "Thy foot shall *not* stumble!" Jesus is now "upholding all things by the word of His power"; shall our unbelief make us the exception? Shall we not rather say, "Uphold *me,* according to Thy word"?

Hebrews 1:3
Matthew 13:58
Psalm 119:116

> Look away to Jesus,
> Look away from all!
> Then we shall not stumble,
> Then we need not fall.

FOURTEENTH DAY.

Thine.

"I am Thine."—Psalm 119:94.

1 Samuel 17:50

THIS is a wonderful stone for the sling of faith. It will slay any Goliath of temptation, if we only sling it out boldly and determinately at him.

When self tempts us (and we know how often that is), let it be met with "Not your own," and then look straight away to Jesus with "I am *Thine.*"

1 Cor. 6:19
Hebrews 12:2
Acts 20:35
John 15:19

If the world tries some lure, old or new, remember the words of the Lord Jesus, how He said: "If ye were of the world, the world would love his own; … but I have chosen you out of the world"; and lest the world should claim us as "his own," look away to Jesus, and say, "I am Thine."

John 17:16

Is it sin, subtle and strong and secret, that claims our obedience? Acknowledge that "ye *were* the servants of sin"; but now, "being made free from sin, ye became the servants of righteousness," and conquer with the faith-shout, "I am *Thine!*"

Romans 6:17, 18

Is it a terrible hand-to-hand fight with Satan himself, making a desperate effort to reassert his old power? Tell the prince of this world that he hath *nothing* in Jesus, and that you are "in Him that is true," a member of His body, His very own; and see if he is not forced to flee at the sound of your confident "I am Thine!"

Revelation 12:12

John 14:30
1 John 5:20
1 Cor. 12:27
Ephesians 5:30
James 4:7

But after all, "I am Thine" is only an echo, varying in clearness according to faith's atmosphere and our nearness to the original voice. Yes, it is only the echo of "Thou art Mine," falling in its mighty music on the responsive, because Spirit-prepared, heart. This note of heavenly music never originated with any earthly rock. It is only when God sends forth the Spirit of His Son in our hearts that we

Isaiah 43:1
Isaiah 44:3–5

Gal 4:6; Rm 8:15

Thine. 37

<small>Jeremiah 3:19
1 Chron. 12:17, 18</small>

<small>John 17:9, 10</small>

<small>Psalm 116:16
Eph. 5:1; 2 Tim. 2:4; Isaiah 35:10
Jn 10:4; Isa 43:10
John 15:14
Luke 1:38</small>

<small>Song. 2:8</small>

<small>Song. 5:1, 2</small>

<small>Isaiah 1:2, 3;
63:8, 10; Mal. 3:6
Numbers 23:19
2 Samuel 7:24
Hosea 2:19
Jeremiah 31:3</small>

<small>Rom 14:8; Acts 27:23; Matt 20:15
Psalm 138:8
Philippians 1:6
Psalm 119:94</small>

cry, "Abba, Father." It was when the anointed but not yet openly crowned king had gone out to meet Amasai, and the Spirit came upon him, that he said, "Thine are we, David." Therefore do not overlook the Voice, in the gladness of the echo. Listen, and you will hear it falling from the mysterious heights of high-priestly intercession: "They are Thine. And all Mine are Thine, and Thine are Mine."

This is no vague and general belonging to Christ, but full of specific realities of relationship. "I am Thine" means, "Truly I am Thy servant." I am one of Thy "dear children." I am Thy chosen soldier. I am Thy ransomed one. I am Thy "own sheep." I am Thy witness. I am Thy friend. And all these are but amens to His own condescending declarations. He says we are all these, and we have only to say, "Yes, Lord, so I am." Why should we ever contradict Him?

In deeper humility and stronger faith let us listen further to the voice of our Beloved, as He breathes names of incomprehensible condescension and love. Shall we contradict Him *here,* in the tenderest outflow of His divine affection, and say, "Not so, Lord"? Shall we not rather adoringly listen, and let Him say even to us in our depths of utter unworthiness, "My sister, My spouse," "My love, My dove, My undefiled," answering only with a wondering, yet unquestioning, "I *am* Thine," "I am all that Thou choosest to say that I am"?

The echo may vary and falter (though it is nothing short of atrocious ingratitude and unbelief when it does), but the Voice never varies or falters. He does not say, "Thou art Mine" to-day, and reverse or weaken it tomorrow. We are "a people unto Thee *for ever,*" and why grieve His love by doubting His word, and giving way to a very fidget of faithlessness? Love that is everlasting *cannot* be ephemeral; it *is* everlasting, and what can we say more?

The more we by faith and experience realize that we are His own in life and death, the more willing we shall be that He should do what He will with His own, and the more sure we shall be that He will do the very best with it, and make the very most of it. May we increasingly find the strength and rest of this our God-given claim upon God. "I am

> Thine, save me!" And "He will save, He will rejoice over thee with joy; He will rest in His love."

Zephaniah 3:17

> "Not your own!" but His ye are,
>   Who hath paid a price untold
> For your life, exceeding far
>   All earth's store of gems and gold.
> With the precious blood of Christ,
> Ransom-treasure all unpriced,
> Full redemption is procured,
> Full salvation is assured.
>
> "Not your own!" but His by right,
>   His peculiar treasure now,
> Fair and precious in His sight,
>   Purchased jewels for His brow.
> He will keep what thus He sought,
> Safely guard the dearly bought,
> Cherish that which He did choose,
> Always love and never lose.

FIFTEENTH DAY.

Unto Thee For Ever.

"What one nation in the earth is like Thy people, even like Israel, whom God went to redeem for a people to Himself, and to make Him a name, and to do for you great things and terrible, for Thy land, before Thy people, which Thou redeemedst to Thee from Egypt, from the nations and their gods? For Thou hast confirmed to Thyself Thy people Israel to be a people unto Thee for ever: and Thou, Lord, art become their God."
—2 Samuel 7:23, 24.

ONE thought, containing three thoughts, seems to pervade this epitome of the history of God's people. The one thought is "Unto Thee!" The three thoughts contained in it are—Redeemed, Separated, Confirmed unto Thee.

Let us take them in order. 1. God "went to redeem" His people. It was no easy sitting still, no costless fiat: "Thou *wentest forth* for the salvation of Thy people, even for salvation with Thine anointed." These "goings forth have been from of old, from the days of eternity," and we have seen by faith these "goings of my God, my King."

Hab. 3:13
Micah 5:2, margin
Psalm 68:24

It was not only to purchase them out of bondage and death, as one might buy a captive thrush on a winter evening, and let it loose into the hungry cold, and think no more about it; it was to redeem them unto Himself, to be His own portion and inheritance and treasure and delight, to be a "people near unto Him," to be the objects on which all His divine love might be poured out, to be the very opportunity of His joy.

Deut. 32:9
Psalm 135:4; 149:4; 148:14
Zephaniah 3:17

His glory and our good were inseparably joined in it. He did it "to make Him a name"; and we may reverently say, that even the very Name which is above every name could not have been the crown of the exaltation of the Son of God but for this.

Philippians 2:9

He also did it because He would "do *for you* great things and terrible,"—great things in mercy, "terrible things in righteousness,"—bringing all His sublimely balanced attributes to bear on His great work "for *you*." "*Before* His people," that we might see, and know, and believe, and praise.

2. This redemption to Himself necessarily involved separation "from Egypt, from the nations and their gods." We cannot have the "to" without the "from," any more than we could go to the equator and not come away from the arctic regions. And the test and proof of the "to Thee" lies in the "from Egypt." But what do we want with Egypt? what is there to attract us to the house of bondage and its old taskmasters? Did we not have enough of them? and shall we not gratefully accept redemption "from the nations," "*out of*" them, from the tyranny of "the customs of the people," "from our vain conversation," and say henceforth, "Thy people shall be my people"? "What have *I* to do any more with idols," when God Himself has redeemed me "from their gods?" Yes, *has* redeemed me, for He says so. "Sing, O ye heavens; for the Lord hath done it!" He "gave Himself for us, that He might redeem us from all iniquity."

3. How magnificently God seals all His transactions! So He has not only redeemed and separated us unto Himself, but "Thou hast *confirmed to Thyself* Thy people Israel." He, not we. His hands laid the foundation, and His hands shall also finish it. He stablisheth us in Christ, and He "hath also sealed us." He "shall also confirm you to the end"; your life shall be one great Confirmation Day of continual defending and strengthening and blessing; He avouching you this day and every day to be His peculiar people, "as He hath promised," and establishing you an holy people unto Himself, and you avouching the Lord to be your God and to walk in His ways.

Not "this day" only, for we are confirmed to Him "to be a people unto Thee for ever." "Thine for ever!" "For I know that whatsoever God doeth, it shall be for ever"; so, having done this, it must be "for ever!" Fling this at the enemy when he tempts you to doubt your complete and eternal redemption—"Unto Thee for ever!" when he tempts

Leviticus 20:26
1 Thess. 3:13;
5:23, 24
2 Thess. 3:3
2 Samuel 7:25

you to regret or tamper with your separation—"Unto Thee for ever!" when he tempts you to quiver about your confirmation "to the end'—"Unto Thee *for ever!*"

For "the Lord is faithful." "And now, O Lord God, the word that Thou hast spoken … establish it for ever, and do as Thou hast said."

> In full and glad surrender,
>   I give myself to Thee,
> Thine utterly and only,
>   And evermore to be.
> O Son of God, who lovest me,
>   I will be Thine alone,
> And all I have and all I am
>   Shall henceforth be Thine own.

SIXTEENTH DAY.

Captive Thoughts.

"Bringing into captivity every thought to the obedience of Christ."—2 Corinthians 10:5.

Psalm 119:113
Jeremiah 4:14

ARE there any tyrants more harassing than our own thoughts? Control of deeds and words seems a small thing in comparison; but have we not been apt to fancy that we really "can't help" our thoughts? Instead of our dominating them, they have dominated us; and we have not expected, nor even thought it possible, to be set free from the manifold tyranny of vain thoughts, and still less of wandering thoughts. Yet, all the time, *here* has been God's word about this hopeless, helpless matter, only *where* has been our faith?

Luke 8.25

It is very strong language that the inspiring Spirit uses here—not "thoughts" in general, but definitely, and with no room for distressing exceptions, "*every* thought." Must it not be glorious rest to have *every* thought of day and night brought into sweet, quiet, complete captivity to Jesus, entirely "obedient to the faith," to His holy and loving influence, to His beautiful and perfect law? We should not have dared to hope or dream of such a rest unto our souls; we should not have guessed it included in that promise to those who take the yoke of Christ upon them; and if we could find one text stating that it was not any part of God's infinitely gracious purposes for us, we should only say, "Of course, for it stands to reason it could not be!"

Psalm 94:19

Acts 6:7
Psalm 19:7
Matthew 11:29

Proverbs 16:3
Isaiah 1:19; 7:9
Philippians 4:19
Matthew 9:29

To reason perhaps, but not to faith; for words cannot be plainer than these in which St. Paul sets forth this marvellous privilege not of himself personally, but of all God's children, if they are only willing and simply believing in the matter. For while "the riches of His glory in Christ Jesus" is the measure of the fulness of His promises, "according to your faith" is the appointed measure of their reception and benefit by ourselves. "Lord, increase *our* faith."

But there is an order in their effectual working, and we must not begin at the wrong end. Before this triumph-leading of every thought can take place, there is the "casting down imaginations," or, as in the more correct margin, "reasonings." As long as we are reasoning about a promise, we never know its reality. It is not God's way. It is the humble who hear thereof and are glad. Have we not found it so? Did we *ever* receive the powerful fulfilment of *any* promise so long as we argued and reasoned, whether with our own hearts or with others, and said, "How can these things be?" Has it not always been, that we had to lay down our arms and accept God's thought and God's way instead of our own ideas, and be willing that He should "speak the word only," and believe it as little children believe our promises? Then, *never* till then, the promise and the privilege became ours not only in potentiality but in actuality. Now, how is it that we do not *yet* understand, and apply the same principle to every promise or privilege which as yet we see only afar off? It is the old way and the only way: "Who through faith … obtained promises."

It is a solemn thought that the alternative of "the obedience of Christ" is disobedience. Thoughts that are not brought into the one are in the other for "the thought of foolishness is *sin*," nothing less or lighter; and when the Holy Spirit "declareth unto man what is his thought," unsuspected sin and unrecognised guilt come terribly to light. But "how long shall thy vain thoughts lodge within thee?" The Conqueror, the always triumphing Saviour, stands at the door and knocks; shall we not "open unto Him *immediately*," and *now* cast down the reasonings which hinder His present triumph, and yield up to Him "who alone *can* order them" the unruly will and affections, and deliver into His victorious hands, the unmanageable thought-garrison (reserving no private slaves, who would quickly again become our masters), and then let Him dwell in our hearts by faith as absolute Captain of our salvation? Then He will garri-

Philippians 4:7 — son our hearts with the peace of God which passeth all understanding.

> Let every thought
> Be captive brought,
> Lord Jesus Christ, to Thine own sweet obedience!
> That I may know,
> In ebbless flow,
> The perfect peace of full and pure allegiance.

SEVENTEENTH DAY.

The Imagination of the Thoughts of the Heart.

"Keep this for ever in the imagination of the thoughts of the heart of Thy people, and prepare (margin, *stablish*) their heart unto Thee."—1 Chronicles 29:18.

Genesis 6:5

Romans 3:24

1 Chron. 29:5
1 Chron. 29:9

1 Chron. 29:14

1 Chr. 29:10–19
Romans 8:34
1 Peter 2:5

Romans 6:13
Romans 12:1

Jeremiah 17:9
Proverbs 28:26

THE words are probably more familiar to us in another connection: "And God saw ... that every imagination of the thoughts of his heart was only evil continually." There is Satan's work through the fall; now let us look at God's work through the redemption that is in Christ Jesus.

What was to be kept for ever in the imagination of the thoughts of the heart? Something that God had put there; for you cannot keep a thing in any place till it is first put there. The people had responded to the appeal of their king, "Who then is willing to consecrate his service this day unto the Lord?" As the expression of this service, they had offered willingly and rejoicingly to the Lord. What they had offered was all His own: "Of thine own have we given Thee." And David acknowledges that it was all of Him that they were enabled (margin, *obtained strength*) "to offer so willingly after this sort." Was all this consecration and joy to be a thing of a day? Nay! in his grand inspired prayer, David, foreshadowing the Royal Intercessor, by whom alone we "offer up spiritual sacrifices," prays, "O Lord God, keep this *for ever* in the imagination of the thoughts of the heart of Thy people."

Now, does not this precisely meet the fear, the desire, and the need of our souls? I may have yielded myself unto God to-day, I may have sincerely presented myself a living sacrifice to Him to-day, but what about to-morrow? My heart is so treacherous, I dare not trust it, I cannot even know it. Who that has consecrated himself to the Lord has not had some such thought! In too many instances, the thought is brooded over till it grows into doubt of His power; and then, of course, we begin to sink, for only by faith do we stand or walk in the bright path of consecration. Doubt indulged soon becomes doubt realized.

He who by His free grace and mighty power put it into our hearts must be equally willing and able to keep it there. If He can keep it there for one day,—nay, for one hour,—He can keep it—how long? Two days? A whole year? What saith the Scripture? *"For Ever."* Yes, but He only; not ourselves. We cannot "keep" it one minute. The more totally we distrust our own ability to put or to keep any right thing whatever in our minds, the more we shall see that we may and must totally trust His power.

There is real comfort in knowing that *every* imagination of the thoughts of the natural heart is *only* evil continually, because this shows how really He is working in us when we find Him putting and keeping holy things in our minds. We may be quite sure no Godward thought comes natural to us; but His new covenant is: "I will put My laws into their mind, and write them in their hearts."

The words are very remarkable and far-reaching. We feel that they go to the very depths, that it is our *whole* mental being which is to be thus pervaded with the incense of consecration; not that it is to be kept only in some inner recess of the heart, and not equally so in the mental consciousness. "Keep this for ever in the *imagination*," so that the mind (margin, imagination) may be stayed on Thee, and the keeping in perfect peace may result. Just the very thing that seems most curbless, the mental lightning that seems too quick for us! The flashing wings that used to bear us too swiftly whither we would not, shall be folded over the golden purpose of consecration. "In the imagination of the *thoughts*." "Bringing into captivity every thought to the obedience of Christ." And then the peace of God enters in to garrison the heart and *thoughts* (for it is the same word, here translated "mind"). "In the imagination of the thoughts of the *heart,*" the very central self, the inner citadel of the soul. *That* shall be "established with grace," stablished unblameable in holiness, "fixed" so that it shall sing and give praise; for Thou, Lord, "hast heard the desire of the humble: Thou wilt establish their heart."

    We rejoice in His omniscience; for, because "the Lord searcheth all hearts, and understandeth all the imaginations of the thoughts," we are fully persuaded that what He has promised He is able also to perform.

> "Only for Jesus!" Lord, keep it for ever
>   Sealed on the heart and engraved on the life;
> Pulse of all gladness, and nerve of endeavour,
>   Secret of rest, and the strength of our strife.

Margin notes: Psalm 10:17, margin; 1 Chron. 28:9; Romans 4:21

EIGHTEENTH DAY.

The Everlasting Service.

"And he shall serve him for ever."—Exodus 21:6.

A PROMISE only differenced from a threat by one thing, love! But that makes all the difference.

Colossians 1:21
Luke 19:14
Ephesians 2:16
2 Cor. 5:17, 14

To those who are still "enemies in their minds," the prospect of serving for ever would be anything but pleasant. But when the enmity is slain by the cross of Christ, and all things are become new, and the love of Christ constraineth, then it is among the brightest of our many bright anticipations, and everlasting joy and everlasting service become almost synonymous.

Proverbs 27:18;
2 Chron. 17:19

Rest is sweet, but service (in proportion to our love) is sweeter still. Those who have served much here cannot but anticipate the fuller and more perfect service above. Those who have to do little more than "stand and wait" here, will perhaps revel even more than others in the new experience of active service, coming at once, as it were, into its full delight.

Exodus 21:2

The Hebrew servant had trial of his master's service for six years, and in the seventh he might go out free if he would. But then, "if the servant shall plainly say" (plainly, avowedly, no mistake about it), "I love my master, ... I *will* not go out free," then, publicly and legally, he was sealed to his service "for ever." It all depended on the love. He would say, "I will not go away from thee; because he loveth thee and thine house, because he is well with thee."

Exodus 21:5

Deut. 15:16

Hebrews 3:6
1 Peter 2:5
1 John 3:14

How this meets our case, dear fellow-servants! We do not want to "go away from" Jesus, because we love Him; and we love His house too,—not only "the house of God" with which so much of our service is connected, but "His own house," the "spiritual house," "the blessed company of all faithful people."

The Everlasting Service.

Psalm 119:65

John 15:27
Isaiah 63:9
Psalm 107:1, 2
Luke 19:40

1 Peter 4:2

Exodus 21:6

Revelation 22:3

Luke 20:36

Revelation 7:15
Malachi 1:13
Isaiah 32:4

1 Cor. 13:12;
Revelation 22:4

John 14:2
Ephesians 2:10

And are we not "well" with Him? Where else so well? where else anything but *ill*? Has He not dealt well with His servants? What a chorus it would be if we all spoke out, and said, "I love my Master, and it hath been well for me with Him"! Why *don't* we speak out, and let people know what a Master He is, and what a happy service His is? Who is to speak out, if *we* have not a word to say about it! Let us stand up for Jesus and His service, every one of us!

Perhaps, when we do speak out, we shall realize the joy of this promise as never before. It was not till the servant had owned his love, and given up "the rest of his time in the flesh," and had his ear bored, that the word was spoken, "He shall serve him for ever"; and it is only the loving and consecrated heart that leaps up for joy at the heavenly prospect: "And His servants shall serve Him."

Think about it a little. What will it be to be able at last to express not only all the love we now feel, but all the perfected love of infinitely enlarged capability of loving in the equally perfected service of equally enlarged capability of serving?—able to show Jesus a love which would burst our hearts if poured into them now! Able to put all the new rapture of praise into living action for Him! Able to go on serving Him day and night, without any weariness in it, and never a hateful shadow of weariness of it; without any interruptions; without any mistakes at all; without any thinking how much better some one else could have done it, or how much better we ought to have done it; above all, without the least mixture of sin in motive or deed—pure, perfect service of Him whom we love and see face to face! What *can* be more joyful?

We are not told much about it, we could not understand it now; the secrets of this wonderful service will only be told when we are brought to His house above, and see what are the heavenly "good works which God hath before ordained" (margin, *prepared*) for us.

How full of surprises the new service will be!—new powers, new and entirely congenial fellow-workers, new spheres, new ministries; only two things not new, if our earthly service has been true,—no new power, and no new

Colossians 1:11
1 Cor. 10:31
Psalm 22:30
Matthew 6:13
Acts 27:23

end and aim, but the same, even His power and His glory! Then shall come the full accomplishment of the Messianic prophecy: "A seed *shall* serve Him"; and still we shall say (only I think we shall *sing* it), "Thine is the kingdom, and the power, and the glory, for ever. Amen." "Whose I am, and whom I serve" *for ever!*

> My Lord hath met my longing
> With word of golden tone,
> That I shall serve for ever
> Himself, Himself alone.
> "Shall serve him,"—and "for ever!"
> Oh hope most sure, most fair!
> The perfect love outpouring,
> In perfect service there!

NINETEENTH DAY.

Most Blessed For Ever.

"Thou hast made him most blessed for ever, Thou hast made him exceeding glad with Thy countenance."—Psalm 21:6.

PROBABLY every one who reads this has at least one of those golden links to heaven which God's own hand has forged from our earthly treasures. It may be that the very nearest and dearest that had been given are now taken away. And how often "no relation, only a dear friend" is an "only" of heart-crushing emphasis!

Ezekiel 24:16;
Job 1:21
Proverbs 18:24
2 Samuel 1:26
Genesis 37:35
Jeremiah 31:15
2 Cor. 1:4
Isaiah 66:13
Revelation 14:13

Human comfort goes for very little in this; but let us lay our hearts open to the comfort wherewith we are comforted of God Himself about it.

There is not much directly to ourselves; He knew that the truest and sweetest comfort would come by looking not at our loss, but at their gain.

Philippians 1:21

Whatever this gain is, it is all His own actual and immediate doing. "*Thou* hast made him" (read here the name of the very one for whom we are mourning) "most blessed."

Matthew 5:3–12;
Numbers 22:6;
Eph. 1:3; Isaiah 30:18; etc., etc.

"Most!" How shall we reach that thought? Make a shining stairway of every bright beatitude in the Bible, blessed upon blessed, within and also far beyond our own experience. And when we have built them up till they reach unto heaven, still this "*most* blessed" is beyond, out of our sight, in the unapproachable glory of God Himself. It will always be "most," for it is "for ever'—everlasting light without a shadow, everlasting songs without a minor.

Isaiah 60:19
Isaiah 35:10
Revelation 21:4
Isaiah 33:24
Isaiah 60:20
Job 3:17, 18; 11:16
Isaiah 65:16;
Revelation 7:17

No more death, neither sorrow nor crying, neither shall there be any more pain. "And the inhabitant shall not say, I am sick." No more sunsets, no more days of mourning. The troubling of the wicked and the voice of the oppressor ceased for ever. No more memory of troubles; no more tears. No more anything that defileth! All this only the negative side of our dear one's present blessedness.

Then, the rest for the weary one, the keeping of the sabbath that remaineth, and yet the service free and perfect and perpetual. The crowns of life, of righteousness, and of glory. The great reward in heaven, full of love-surprise to the consciously unprofitable servant. The far more exceeding weight of glory borne by some to whom the grasshopper had been a burden.

The scene of all the blessedness,—the better country, the continuing city, the King's palace, the Father's house, the prepared mansions (perhaps full of contrasts to the past pilgrimage),—all summed up in the transcendent simplicity and sublimity of His words, "That where I am, *there* ye may be also."

The music! What will all the harps of heaven be to the thrill of the One Voice, saying, "Come, ye blessed of my Father!" and, "Well done, good and faithful servant, enter thou into the joy of thy Lord." Our dear ones *have heard that!* and that one word of the King must have made them *most* blessed for ever.

But more yet. "Thou hast made him exceeding glad with thy countenance." "Hast," for it is done. At this moment they *are* exceeding glad, and the certainty of it stills every quiver of our selfish love. The glory and joy of our Lord Christ are revealed to them, and they are "glad also with exceeding joy," rejoicing together with Jesus.

How can they help reflecting His Divine joy when they see it no longer by faith and afar off, but visibly, actually "face to face!" nay, more, "eye to eye," that very closest approach of tenderest intercourse too deep for words. They see Him "as He is"; in all His beauty and love and glory; through no veil, no glass, no tear-mist.

The prayer for them, "The Lord lift up His countenance upon thee," is altogether fulfilled, and they are "full of joy with Thy countenance." And *every* other prayer we ever prayed for them is fulfilled exceeding abundantly, above all we asked or thought. We may not pray any more for them, because God has not left one possibility of blessedness un-bestowed.

> "Breaking the narrow prayers that may
> Befit your narrow hearts, away
> In His broad, loving will."
>
> E. B. BROWNING.

Psalm 43:4
Matthew 11:26

God Himself, their exceeding joy, has done and is doing His very best for them. "Even so, Father!"

> For I know
> That they who are not lost, but gone before,
> Are only waiting till I come; for death
> Has only parted us a little while,
> And has not severed e'en the finest strand
> In the eternal cable of our love:
> The very strain has twined it closer still,
> And added strength. The music of their lives
> Is nowise stilled, but blended so with songs
> Around the throne of God, that our poor ears
> No longer hear it.

TWENTIETH DAY.

Do Thou for Me.

"Do Thou for Me."—Psalm 109:21

THE Psalmist does not say what he wanted God to do for him. He leaves it open. So this most restful prayer is left open for all perplexed hearts to appropriate "according to their several necessities." And so we leave it open for God to fill up in His own way.

Only a trusting heart can pray this prayer at all: the very utterance of it is an act of faith. We could not ask any one whom we did not know intimately and trust implicitly to "do" for us, without even suggesting what.

Only a self-emptied heart can pray it. It is when we have come to the end of our own resources, or rather, come to see that we never had any at all, that we are willing to accept the fact that we can "do nothing," and to let God do everything for us.

Only a loving heart can pray it. For nobody likes another to take them and their affairs in hand, and "do" for them, unless that other is cordially loved. We might submit to it, but we should not like it, and certainly should not seek it.

So, if we have caught at this little prayer as being just what we want, just what it seems a real rest to say, I think it shows that we do trust in Him and not in ourselves, and that we do love Him really and truly. There is sure to be a preface to this prayer. "Neither know *we* what to do." Perhaps we have been shrinking from being brought to this. Rather let us give thanks for it. It is the step down from the drifting wreck on to the ladder still hanging at the side. Will another step be down into the dark water? Go on, a little lower still, fear not! The next is, "We know not what

Margin references:
Deut. 32:36
Psalm 109:22
John 15:5

Joshua 9:25

1 Cor. 1:9

2 Chron. 20:12

2 Cor. 12:9, 10

Romans 8:26

Do Thou for Me.

2 Chron. 13:12; 14:11	we should pray for." Now we have reached the lowest step. What next? "Do Thou for me." This is the step into the captain's boat. Now He will cut loose from the wreck of our efforts, ladder and all will be left behind, and we have nothing to do but to "sit still" and let Him take us to our "desired haven," probably steering quite a different course from anything we should have thought best. Not seldom "*immediately* the ship is at the land whither" we went.
Ruth 3:18 Psalm 107:30 John 6:21	
Job 23:13	What may we, from His own word, expect in answer to this wide petition? 1. "What His soul desireth, even that He doeth." Contrast this with our constantly felt inability to do a hundredth part of what we desire to do for those we love. Think of what God's desires must be for us, whom He so loves, that He spared not His own Son. "*That* He doeth!"
Romans 8:32 Job 23:14 Romans 8:3, 4 Ephesians 1:3–12 1 Thess. 5:9, etc. Ephesians 2:10 Acts 22:10 Philippians 2:13 Isaiah 26:12	2. "He performeth the thing that is appointed for me." This is wonderfully inclusive; one should read over all the epistles to get a view of the things present and future, seen and unseen, the grace and the glory that He has appointed for us. It includes also all the "good works which God hath before ordained, that we should walk in them." It will not be our performance of them, but His; for He "worketh in you to will and to do," and "Thou also hast wrought all our works in us."
Psalm 57:2	3. The beautiful old translation says, He "shall perform the cause which I have in hand." Does not that make it very real to us to-day? Just the very thing that "I have in hand," my own particular bit of work to-day,—this cause that I cannot manage, this thing that I undertook in miscalculation of my own powers, *this* is what I may ask Him to do "for me, and rest assured that He will perform it." "The wise and their works are in the hand of God!"
Romans 4:21 Eccles. 9:1 Psalm 57:2	
Romans 15:4	4. He "performeth all things for me." Does He mean as much as this? Well, He has caused it to be written for us "that we might have hope"; and what more do we want? Then *let* Him do it. *Let* Him perform all things for us.
1 Cor. 3:12–15	Not some things, but *all* things; or the very things which we think there is no particular need for Him to perform will be all failures—wood, hay, and stubble to be burnt up. One by one let us claim this wonderful word; "the

1 Kings 8:59, margin	thing of a day in his day," "as the matter shall require," being always brought to Him with the God-given petition, "Do thou for me."
Isaiah 38:14	Do not wait to feel very much "oppressed" before you say, "O Lord, undertake for me." Far better say that at first than at last, as we have too often done! Bring the prayer in one hand, and the promises in the other, joining them in
2 Samuel 7:25	the faith-clasp of "Do as Thou hast said!" And put both
John 11:42	the hands into the hand of Him whom the Father heareth always, saying, "Do Thou for me, O Lord God, for Thy
Isaiah 9:6	name's sake," for the sake of Jehovah-Jesus, the mighty God, the everlasting Father, yet the Saviour of sinners.

TWENTY-FIRST DAY.

Marvellously helped.

"Marvellously helped."—2 Chronicles 26:15.

2 Chron. 26: 9–15

UZZIAH seems to have been the type of a variously busy and successful man. He had all sorts of irons in the fire. So many energetic interests and tastes, with both faculty and opportunity for developing them, must have made his life much more agreeable and lively than most royal careers. His architecture and his agriculture, his war or-

2 Chron. 26:8
2 Chron. 26:5
2 Chron. 26:21

ganizations and his engineering, spread his name far abroad. For "as long as he sought the Lord, God made him to prosper." Yet the end of his story is a strange contrast,—a leper, dwelling in a several house, and cut off from the house of the Lord.

2 Chron. 27:8; cf. 12:1; Ps. 30:7
Jeremiah 17:5
2 Cor. 12:10

Where was the turning-point? Probably in the words, "He strengthened *himself* exceedingly." It had been God's help and strength before, and he had risen very high. Then he thought he was strong, and he was brought fearfully low.

"Marvellously helped *till* he was strong." Then who would not be always weak, that they might be always "marvellously helped!"

"Marvellously!" For is it not wonderful that God should help us at all? Have we not wondered hundreds of times at the singular help He has given? If we have not, what ungrateful blindness! For he has been giving it ever since we

Psalm 71:6, P.B.V.

were helpless babies. "Through Thee have I been holden up ever since I was born." How much of His help has been forgotten or altogether unnoticed.

Luke 12.7

The very little things, the microscopical helpings, often seem most marvellous of all, when we consider that it was Jehovah Himself who stooped to the tiny need of a moment. And the greater matters prove themselves to be the Lord's

Psalm 118:23

doing, just because they are so marvellous in our eyes.

Ps. 33:20; Zech. 3:8; Psalm 71:7

Why should we fear being brought to some depth of perplexity and trouble when we know He will be true to His name, and be "our Help," so that we shall be even "men wondered at" because so marvellously helped!

Psalm 49:20
Job 9:10
Psalm 40:5
1 Samuel 12:24

It is not a mere expression. The Bible always means what it says; and so the help to Uzziah, and the same help with which God makes us to prosper, is literally "marvellous." We do wonder at it, or ought to wonder at it. Wonder is one of the God-given faculties which distinguish us from the beasts that perish. And He gives us grand scope for its happy exercise not merely in His works in general, but in His dealings with us in particular. But wonder is always founded upon observation. We do not wonder at that which we do not observe. So, if we have not wondered very much at the help He has given us, it is because we have not noticed, not considered very much, how great things He hath done for us.

2 Kings 6:17
Joel 2:26

Let us turn our special attention to it each day. We are wanting help of all kinds all day long; now just observe how He gives it! Even if nothing the least unusual happens, the *opened* and *watching* eye will see that the whole day is one sweet story of marvellous help. And perhaps the greatest marvel will be, that He has helped us to *see* His help after very much practical blindness to it. And then the marvelling will rise into praising "the name of the Lord your God, that hath dealt wondrously with you."

Deut. 8:10–14
2 Chron. 26:16
Numbers 22:38
Deut. 32:36; Isaiah 59:16
Ps. 121:2; 40:17; 33:20; 46:1
Daniel 11:34

The times of marvellous help are times of danger. "When thou hast eaten and art full, ... and all that thou hast is multiplied," "beware lest" "*then* thy heart be lifted up." "*When* he was strong, his heart was lifted up to his destruction." Unclasp the ivy from the elm, and it is prostrate at once. Thank God, if He keeps us realizing, amidst the busiest work, and the pleasantest success, that we have no power *at all* of ourselves to help ourselves! Then there will be nothing to hinder His "continual help." As long as we say quite unreservedly, "My help cometh from the Lord," the help will come. As long as we are saying, "Thou art my help," "He *is* our help," "a very present help." Then we shall not "be holpen with a *little* help," which is too often all we

Isaiah 40:29
2 Chron. 20:12
John 21:7
Matt. 14:30, 31
2 Cor. 12:9

really expect from our omnipotent Helper, just because we do not feel that we have "*no* might." Peter was a good swimmer, but he did not say, "Lord, help me to swim!" He said, "Lord, *save* me!" and so the Master's help was instant and complete. "Most gladly therefore will I rather glory in my infirmities, that the power of Christ may rest upon me."

> The Lord *hath* done great things for thee!
>   All through the fleeted days
> Jehovah hath dealt wondrously;
>   Lift up thy heart and praise!
> For greater things thine eyes shall see,
>   Child of His loving choice!
> The Lord *will* do great things for thee;
>   Fear not, be glad, rejoice!

TWENTY-SECOND DAY.

Thou understandest.

"Thou understandest my thought."—Psalm 139:2.

WHO does not know what it is to be misunderstood? Perhaps no one ever is always and perfectly understood, because so few Christians are like their Master in having the spirit of "*quick* understanding." But this does not make it the less trying to you; and you do not feel able to say with St. Paul, "With me it is a very small thing." But this precious Word, which meets every need, gives you a stepping-stone which is quite enough to enable you to reach that brave position, if you will only stand on it. "*Thou* understandest my thought."

Even if others "daily mistake" your words, He understands your thought, and is not this infinitely better? He Himself, your ever-loving, ever-present Father, understands. He understands perfectly just what and just when others do not. Not your actions merely, but your thought—the central self which no words can reveal to others. "All my desire is before Thee." He understands how you desired to do the right thing when others thought you did the wrong thing. He understands how His poor weak child wants to please Him, and secretly mourns over grieving Him. "Thou understandest" seems to go even a step further than the great comfort of "Thou knowest." "His understanding is infinite."

Perhaps you cannot even understand yourself, saying, "How can a man then understand his own way?" Even this He meets, for "He declareth unto man what is His thought." But are you willing to let Him do this? He may show you that those who have, as you suppose, misunderstood you, may have guessed right after all. He may show you that your desire was not so honest, your motives not so

Isaiah 11:3

1 Cor. 4:3

Psalm 56:5, P.B.V.

1 Chron. 28:9

Psalm 38:9

Joshua 22:22
Psalm 143:10, P.B.V.

Jer. 15:15; Psalm 147:5

Proverbs 20:24
Amos 4:13

Jeremiah 17:9

Luke 11:34; Col. 3:22; Ps. 19:12 Psalm 139:23, 24 1 John 1:7	single as you fancied; that there was self-will where you only recognised resolution, sin where you only recognised infirmity or mistake. *Let* Him search, let Him "declare" it unto you. For then He will declare another message to you: "The blood of Jesus Christ His Son cleanseth us from all sin."
Job 42:1–7 John 21:17 1 John 1:9	Then, when all is clear between Him and you, "nothing between" (and let that "*when*" be "*now!*"), how sweet you will find it in the light of His forgiveness, and the new strength of His cleansing, to look up and say, "*Thou* understandest!" and wait patiently for Him to let you be understood or misunderstood, just as He will, even as Jesus did. For who was ever so misunderstood as He?
Hebrews 4:12, 13 Psalm 38:9 1 Chr. 29:17, 18 Ezekiel 36:25–27	Almighty God, unto whom all hearts be open, all desires known, and from whom no secrets are hid; Cleanse the thoughts of our hearts by the inspiration of Thy Holy Spirit, that we may perfectly love Thee, and worthily magnify Thy holy name, though Christ our Lord. Amen.

TWENTY-THIRD DAY.

The Proof of His Purpose.

"No man can come unto me, except it were given him of my Father."—John 6:65.

Hebrews 6:18

PERHAPS we have hardly counted this as any part of the royal comfort of our King. And yet it is full of "strong consolation."

1 John 2:25

If some of us were asked, "How do you know you have everlasting life?" we might say, "Because God has promised it." But how do you know He has promised it to you? And then if we answered, not conventionally, nor what we think we ought to say, but honestly what we think, we might say,

John 3:16

"Because I have believed and have come to Jesus." And this looks like resting our hope of salvation upon something that we have done, upon the fact of our having consciously believed and consciously "come." And then, of course, any whirlwind of doubt will raise dust enough to obscure that fact and all the comfort of it.

Romans 8:29, 30
Isaiah 26:12

Yet there is grand comfort, not in it, but in the glorious chain of which even this little human link is first forged and then held by Jehovah's own hand. Apart from this, it is worth nothing at all.

Revelation 22:19;
1:5; Matt. 24:35
John 6:60–66

Do not shrink from the words; do not dare to explain them away; the Faithful and True Witness spoke them, the Holy Ghost has recorded them for ever: "No man *can* come unto Me, except it were given unto him of My Father." There it stands; reiterated and strengthened instead of softened, because many even of His disciples murmured

Ephesians 2:8

at it. So our coming to Jesus was not of ourselves; it was the gift of God.

John 6:44
Revelation 22:17

How did the gift operate? Not by driving, but by drawing. "No man can come to Me, except the Father which hath sent Me draw him." Here comes in the great "Whosoever *will.*" For unless and until the Father drew us, no mortal born of Adam ever wanted to come to Jesus. There was nothing else for it; He *had* to draw us, or we never should have thought of wishing to come; nay, we should have gone on distinctly willing *not* to come, remaining aliens and enemies. Oh, the terrible depth of depravity revealed by that keen sword-word, "Ye *will not* come to Me that ye might have life." Settle it, then, that you never wanted to come till He drew you, and praise Him for thus beginning at the very beginning with you. You were not ready for the "whosoever will" before. But no one ever had a glimmer of a *will* to come, but that shining "whosoever" flashed its world-wide splendour for their opening eyes.

By your will, now being wrought upon more and more by His Spirit, the Father drew you, "with cords of a man, with bands of love." Just examine now,—was it not so? was it with anything *but* loving-kindness that He drew you? Remember the way by which He led you; it may have been hedged with thorns, but was it not "paved with love"? were not the very stones laid "with fair colours"? Can you help seeing "the loving-kindnesses of the Lord" all along? and what were they lavished for, but to draw you?

That being acknowledged, what next? Loving-kindness is the fruit and expression and absolute proof of everlasting love. There is no escape from this magnificent conclusion,—"Yea, I have loved thee" (personally *thee*) "with an everlasting love," for "*therefore* with loving-kindness have I drawn thee" (personally *thee*). The coming was personal and individual; it may have been "in the press," but we had nothing to do with the rest of the throng; we know in ourselves that we, you and I, individually, have come. That personal coming was because of God the Father's personal drawing. I do not know how He drew you, you do not know how He drew me; but without it most certainly neither you nor I ever could have come, because we never *would* have come. This personal drawing by personal loving-kindness was because of personal and individual everlasting love. Coming only because drawn, drawn only because loved! Here we reach, and rest on, the firm foundation of the electing love of God

2 Thess. 2:13;
1 Peter 1:2

2 Timothy 2:13

in Christ, proved by His drawing, resulting in our coming! When we know that this sun is shining in the heaven of heavens, should we be watching every flicker of our little farthing candle of faith?

> From no less fountain such a stream could flow,
>   No other root could yield so fair a flower:
> Had He not loved, He had not drawn us so;
>   Had he not drawn, we had nor will nor power
> To rise, to come;—the Saviour had passed by
> Where we in blindness sat without one care or cry.

TWENTY-FOURTH DAY.

The Garnering of the Least Grain.

"I will sift the house of Israel among all nations, like as corn is sifted in a sieve, yet shall not the least grain fall upon the earth."—Amos 9:9.

THERE is double comfort here, as to *others* and as to *ourselves*. As to others,—have not some of us had a scarcely detected notion, as if to some extent the salvation of others depended upon our efforts? Of course, we never put it in so many words; but has there not been something of a feeling that if we tried very hard to win a soul we should succeed, and if we did not try quite enough it would get lost? And this has made our service anxious and burdensome.

John 6:37
Jeremiah 31:3
John 12:32
Romans 8:13
Romans 8:29, 30

Genesis 6:13–16; 6:18
Luke 14:17
Genesis 7:1, 7, 16

But what says Christ? "All that the Father giveth Me shall come to Me." They shall come, for the Father will draw them, and Jesus will attract them, and the Holy Spirit will lead them. And the purpose precedes the promise, even as the promise precedes the call, and the call precedes the coming. Thus God first planned and proposed the ark for the salvation of Noah from the flood. Then He said, "Thou *shalt come* into the ark." Long after that, when all things were ready, He said, "Come thou and all thy house into the ark." And then Noah went in; and then "the Lord shut him in."

Isaiah 43:13
John 6:39

Now let us, in our work, practically trust our Lord as to His purposes, promises, and calls; quite satisfied that He "will work, and who shall let it?" that He will not accidentally miss anybody, or lose anything of all that the Father hath given Him, for this is the Father's own will.

John 17:4
Genesis 18:25

It may seem a great trial of trust very often, but who is it that we have to trust thus unquestioningly and quietly? Jesus Christ! Cannot we trust Him whom the Father trusted with the tremendous work of redemption? Shall He not do right? Cannot we trust the Good Shepherd about His own sheep? Why should it actually seem harder to trust Him about His own affairs than about our own? "Trust in Him at *all* times," includes the time when we almost fancy the salvation of a dear one depends on our little bits of prayers and efforts. Not that this trust will tend to easy-going idleness. It never does this when it is real. The deepest trust leads to the most powerful action. It is the silencing oil that makes the machine obey the motive power with greatest readiness and result.

Then the comfort for ourselves. Satan has desired to have us, that he may sift us as wheat; but the Lord Himself keeps the sieve in His own hand, and pledges His word that not the least grain shall fall on the earth.

We are so glad of that word, "not the *least*"; not even me, though less than the least of all saints, though feeling as if my only claim upon Christ Jesus is that I am the chief of sinners.

"Not the least grain"; for He says, "Ye shall be gathered one by one." Think of His hand gathering you separately and individually out of His million-sheaved harvest; gathering you, one by one always, into His garner, even in that tremendous day of sifting, when He shall thoroughly purge His floor. You may feel a little overlooked sometimes now; only one among so very many, and perhaps not first nor even second in anybody's love, or care, or interest, but He is watching His "least grains" all the time. A flock of sheep look most uninterestingly alike and hopelessly undistinguishable to us, but a good shepherd knows every one quite well. Yes, the Good Shepherd calleth His own sheep by name here, and "in Zion every one of them appeareth before God."

For as He said at first, "All that the Father giveth Me *shall come* to Me"; so He says they "*shall come* from the east and west" to receive the eternal welcome to the great feast of His kingdom; His "sons *shall come* from far," "they *shall come* up with acceptance"; till every one (and that means you and I) has heard His own "Come, ye blessed of my Fa-

1 Cor. 2:9	ther," and has come into the fulness of all that He has prepared for us.
John 17:24	Our Saviour and our King, Enthroned and crowned above,
Jude 24	Shall with exceeding gladness bring
Hebrews 2:13	The children of His love.
	All that the Father gave His glory shall behold;
John 10:16	Not one whom Jesus came to save
John 17:20	Is missing from His fold.

TWENTY-FIFTH DAY.

Vindication.

"And they shall know."—Ezekiel 6:10; 36:38, etc.

Num. 32:6–19
Joshua 22:11–29
Mark 11:5
1 Cor. 4:5

Jude 10

Revelation 13:10
Psalm 139:20, 21
Isaiah 1:2, 3
Psalm 56:5, P.B.V.
Psalm 119:136, 139

1 John 2:13
Ps. 119:126, 127
John 6:66–69
Matt. 16:14–16

Revelation 1:7
Matthew 25:31;
2 Thess. 1:7

Isaiah 51:6–8
Romans 3:4
2 Thess. 1:7–10

"IF they only knew!" How often we say or think this when "they" misunderstand and misjudge a person, a position, or an action, just because "they" do not know what we know! How we chafe against their speaking evil of things which they know not, and most of all when "they" speak wrongly or unworthily of a person whom we know much better than "they" do! Ah, if they only knew!

This grieving sense of the injustice of ignorance rises to a feeling which needs much tempering of faith and patience when we see our God Himself misunderstood and misjudged. Oh, how they "daily mistake" His words and His character, and how it *does* pain us! How we do want them to know what He is, even so far as we are privileged to know Him! How every word which shows they do not know His exceeding great love and absolute goodness, and the sublime balancing of all His attributes, jars upon us and distresses us, and causes a quick up-glance of His little children who have *known* the Father, and an involuntary closer nestling of their hand in His, as if they wanted to give Him fresh assurance of their love and confidence, just because these others do *not* know Him!

What an added grandeur it gives to our anticipations of the day when every eye shall see Him, that He, our Father, will be *known* at last to be what He is, and that Jesus, our Lord and Master, will be seen in His own glory, and can never, never be misunderstood any more! One revels in the thought of this great and eternal vindication of Him whom we love; His ways, His works, His word all justified, and Himself revealed to the silenced universe, henceforth only

Vindication.

<small>Revelation 5:12
Psalm 50:2, 6</small>

to receive honour and glory and blessing! It seems as if we should almost forget our own share in the glory and joy of His coming in this transcendent satisfaction.

"And they *shall* know!" It is one of the shining threads that run all through the Bible, a supply indeed for the heart's desire of those who delight in the Lord. It is never long out of sight, judgments and mercies being alike sent for this great purpose, that men may know that Jehovah is Most High over all the earth. For this the waters of the Red Sea receded and returned again; for this Jordan was dried up; for this Goliath was delivered into David's hand; for this 185,000 of the Assyrians were smitten by God's angel; and many more instances. Throughout Ezekiel it seems the very keyword, recurring seventy-five times as the divine reason of divine doings, that they may "know that I am the Lord." Is there not a peculiar solace in this?

<small>Psalm 37:4
Exodus 9:14
Psalm 83:18
Exodus 14:18, 21
Joshua 4:23, 24
1 Samuel 17:46
Isaiah 37:20, 36
Jeremiah 16:21

Ezekiel 15:7, etc.</small>

His word, too, shall be vindicated, for "ye shall *know* that I the Lord have spoken it."

<small>Ezekiel 17:21</small>

His ways shall be vindicated, for "ye shall *know* that I have not done without cause all that I have done in it." "Thou *shalt* know hereafter."

<small>Ezekiel 14:23

John 13:7</small>

His house shall be vindicated, for He will answer the prayers ascending from it, "that they may *know* that thy name is called upon this house."

<small>1 Kings 8:43, margin</small>

And He will not leave His own children out of the great vindication; for "the hand of the Lord shall be known toward His servants." "All that see them shall acknowledge them, that they are the seed which the Lord hath blessed." More than that, the whole world shall "*know* that Thou hast loved them as Thou hast loved Me," and "I will make them ... to know that I have loved thee." Is not this superabounding compensation for any tiny share we may now have in the world-wide misunderstanding of our Father's wisdom and our Saviour's love?

<small>Ezekiel 2:5; 33:33
Isaiah 66:14
Isaiah 61:9

John 17:23
Revelation 3:9

1 John 3:1
John 15:18–20</small>

"And they shall know," is not only for those who do not know at all; for "at that day *ye* shall know that I am in My Father, and ye in Me, and I in you,"—revelations of the mysteries of Godhead and of the ineffable union of Christ with His people, which have not yet entered into our hearts

<small>John 14:20
John 16:25

1 Cor. 2:9</small>

Hosea 6:3
1 Cor. 13:12

to conceive. "Then shall *we* know (if we follow on to know) the Lord." "For now I know in part; but then shall I know even as also I am known."

> Oh! the joy to see Thee reigning,
>   Thee, my own belovèd Lord!
> Every tongue Thy name confessing,
> Worship, honour, glory, blessing,
>   Brought to Thee with glad accord!
> Thee, my Master and my Friend,
>   Vindicated and enthroned,
> Unto earth's remotest end,
>   Glorified, adored, and owned!

TWENTY-SIXTH DAY.

Wakeful Hours.

"Thou holdest mine eyes waking."—Psalm 77:4.

Psalm 4:8

Psalm 127:2
Isaiah 50:4
Job 7:3

Job 23:14

Psalm 139:5

Philippians 4:19
Psalm 34:9

Job 23:14
Psalm 39:9

Psalm 143:10

IF we could always say, night after night, "I will both lay me down in peace and sleep," receiving in full measure the Lord's quiet gift to His beloved, we should not learn the disguised sweetness of this special word for the wakeful ones. When the wearisome nights come, it is hushing to know that they are appointed. But this is something nearer and closer-bringing, something individual and personal; not only an appointment, but an act of our Father: "Thou *holdest* mine eyes waking." It is *not* that He is merely not giving us sleep; it is not a denial, but a different dealing. Every moment that the tired eyes are sleepless, it is because our Father is holding them waking. It seems so natural to say, "How I wish I could go to sleep!" Yet even that restless wish may be soothed by the happy confidence in our Father's hand, which will not relax its "hold" upon the weary eyelids until the right moment has come to let them fall in slumber.

Ah! but we say, "It is not only *wish*, I really *want* sleep." Well; wanting it is one thing, and needing it is another. For He is pledged to supply "all our *need,* not all our *notions.*" And if He holds our eyes waking, we may rest assured that, so long as He does so, it is not sleep but wakefulness that is our true need.

Now, if we first simply submit ourselves to the appointed wakefulness, instead of getting fidgeted because we cannot go to sleep, the resting in His will, even in this little thing, will bring a certain blessing. And the perfect learning of this little page in the great lesson-book of our Father's will, will make others easier and clearer.

Then, let us remember that He does nothing without a purpose, and that no dealing is meant to be resultless. So it is well to pray that we may make the most of the wakeful hours, that they may be no more wasted ones than if we were up and dressed. They are His hours, for "the night also is Thine." It will cost no more mental effort (nor so much) to ask Him to let them be holy hours, filled with His calming presence, than to let the mind run upon the thousand "other things" which seem to find even busier entrance during night.

> "With thoughts of Christ and things divine
> Fill up this foolish heart of mine."

It is an opportunity for proving the real power of the Holy Spirit to be greater than that of the Tempter. And He will without fail exert it, when sought for Christ's sake. He will teach us to commune with our own heart upon our bed, or perhaps simply to "be still," which is, after all, the hardest and yet the sweetest lesson. He will bring to our remembrance many a word that Jesus has said, and even "the night shall be light about" us in the serene radiance of such rememberings. He will so apply the word of God that the promise shall be fulfilled: "When thou awakest, it shall talk with thee." He will tune the silent hours, and give songs in the night, which shall blend in the Father's ear with the unheard melodies of angels.

Can we say, "With my soul have I desired Thee in the night"? and, "By night on my bed I sought Him whom my soul loveth"? Then He will fulfil that desire; the very wakefulness should be recognised as His direct dealing, and we may say, "Thou hast visited me in the night." It is not an angel that comes to you as to Elijah, and arouses you from slumber, but the Lord of angels. He watches while you sleep, and when you are awake you are still with Him who died for you, that whether you wake or sleep, both literally and figuratively, you should live together with Him.

Margin references:
Psalm 74:16
Mark 4:19
1 John 4:4
Psalm 4:4
John 14:26
Psalm 139:11
Proverbs 6:22
Psalm 42:8
Job 35:10
Isaiah 26:9
Song. 3:1, 4
Psalm 145:19
Psalm 17:3
1 Kings 19:5
Psalm 121:4
Psalm 139:18
1 Thess. 5:10

TWENTY-SEVENTH DAY.

Midnight Rememberings.

"When I remember Thee upon my bed."—Psalm 63:6.

<small>2 Cor. 10:5
Jeremiah 4:14
Psalm 119:113

1 Peter 2:24

John 14:26
Psalm 20:7
e.g. Ex. 34:5–7;
Isaiah 9:6
Psalm 77:10, 11
Song. 1:4
Jeremiah 31:3
John 16:27; 13:1
Ephesians 3:19
Romans 15:30
Philippians 2:1
Deut. 15:15

Job 7:3
Ps. 6:6; Song. 3:1
Psalm 42:6</small>

MEMORY is never so busy as in the quiet time while we are waiting for sleep; and never, perhaps, are we more tempted to useless recollections and idle reveries than "in the night watches." Perhaps we have regretfully struggled against them; perhaps yielded to effortless indulgence in them, and thought we could not help it, and were hardly responsible for "vain thoughts" at such times. But here is full help and bright hope. This night let us "remember Thee." We can only remember what we already know; oh praise Him, then, that we have material for memory!

There is enough for all the wakeful nights of a lifetime in the one word "Thee." It leads us straight to "His own self"; dwelling on that one word, faith, hope, and love, wake up and feed and grow. Then the holy remembrance, wrought by His Spirit, widens. For "we will remember the *name* of the Lord our God," in its sweet and manifold revelations. "I will remember the *years*" and "the *works* of the Lord." "Surely I will remember Thy *wonders* of old." Most of all "we will remember Thy *love*," the everlasting love of our Father, the "exceeding great love of our Master and only Saviour," the gracious, touching love of our Comforter. And the remembrance of all this love will include that of its grand act and proof, "Thou shalt remember that ... Jehovah thy God redeemed thee."

Perhaps we know what it is to feel peculiarly weary-hearted and dispirited "on our beds." But when we say, "O my God, my soul is cast down within me"; let us add at once, "*Therefore* will I remember Thee."

And what then? what comes of thus remembering Him? "My soul" (yes, your soul) "shall be satisfied as with marrow and fatness, and my mouth shall praise Thee with joyful lips: *when* I remember Thee upon my bed, and meditate on Thee in the night watches." What can be a sweeter, fuller promise than this!—our heart's desire fulfilled in abundant satisfaction and joyful power of praise! Yet there is a promise sweeter and more thrilling still to the loving, longing heart. "Thou meetest … those that remember Thee in Thy ways." And so, this very night, as you put away the profitless musings and memories, and remember Him upon your bed, He will keep His word and meet you. The darkness shall be verily the shadow of His wing, for your feeble, yet Spirit-given remembrance, shall be met by His real and actual presence, for "hath He said and shall He not do it?" Let us pray that this night "the desire of our soul" may be "to Thy name, and to *the remembrance of Thee.*"

Psalm 63:5, 6

Psalm 37:4

Psalm 40:3

Isaiah 64:5

Psalm 91:4, 5

Numbers 23:19

Isaiah 26:8

TWENTY-EIGHTH DAY.

The Bright Side of Growing Older.

"And thine age shall be clearer than the noonday; thou shalt shine forth, thou shalt be as the morning."—Job 11:17.

<small>Eccles. 1:4, 5
Eccles. 11:8
Job 9:25
Psalm 90:9, 10</small>

I SUPPOSE nobody ever did naturally like the idea of getting older, after they had at least " left school." There is a sense of oppression and depression about it. The irresistible, inevitable onward march of moments and years without the possibility of one instant's pause—a march that, even while on the uphill side of life, is leading to the downhill side—casts an autumn-like shadow over even many a spring birthday; for perhaps this is never more vividly felt than when one is only passing from May to June,—sometimes earlier still. But how surely the Bible gives us the bright side of everything! In this case it gives three bright sides of a fact, which, without it, could not help being gloomy.

<small>1 John 1:7</small>

First, it opens the sure prospect of *increasing brightness* to those who have begun to walk in the light. Even if the sun of our life has reached the apparent zenith, and we have known a very noonday of mental and spiritual being, it is no poetic "western shadows" that are to lengthen upon our way, but "our age is to be *clearer* than the noonday." How

<small>Job 11:17

Psalm 36:9

Zechariah 14:7</small>

suggestive that word is! The light, though intenser and nearer, shall dazzle less; "in Thy light shall we *see* light," be able to bear much more of it, see it more clearly, see all else by it more clearly, reflect it more clearly. We should have said, "At evening-time there shall be shadow"; God says, "At evening-time there shall be light."

<small>Proverbs 4:18</small>

Also, we are not to look for a very dismal afternoon of life with only some final sunset glow; for He says it "shineth more and more unto the perfect day"; and "more and more" leaves no dark intervals; we are to expect a continually brightening path. "The future is one vista of brightness and blessedness" to those who are willing only to "walk in the light." Just think, when you are seven, or ten, or twenty years older, that will only mean seven, or ten, or twenty years" more experience of His love and faithfulness, more light of the knowledge of the glory of God in the face of Jesus Christ; and *still* the "more and more unto the *perfect day*," will be opening out before us! We are "confident of this very thing!"

The second bright side is *increasing fruitfulness*. Do not let us confuse between works and fruit. Many a saint in the land of Beulah is not able to *do* anything at all, and yet is bringing forth fruit unto God beyond the busiest workers. So that even when we come to the days when "the strong men shall bow themselves," there may be more pleasant fruits for our Master, riper and fuller and sweeter, than ever before. For "they shall still bring forth fruit in old age"; and the man that simply "trusteth in the Lord" "shall not be careful in the year of drought, neither shall cease from yielding fruit."

Some of the fruits of the Spirit seem to be especially and peculiarly characteristic of sanctified older years; and do we not want to bring them *all* forth? Look at the splendid ripeness of Abraham's "faith" in his old age; the grandeur of Moses' "meekness," when he went up the mountain alone to die; the mellowness of St. Paul's "joy" in his later epistles; and the wonderful "gentleness" of St. John, which makes us almost forget his early character of "a son of thunder," wanting to call down God's lightnings of wrath. And "the same Spirit" is given to us, that we too may bring forth "fruit that may abound," and always "more fruit."

The third bright side is brightest of all: "*Even to your old age, I am He*"; always the same Jehovah-Jesus; with us "all the days," bearing and carrying us "all the days"; reiterating His promise—"even to hoar hairs will I carry you ... ; even I will carry and will deliver you," just as He carried the lambs in His bosom. For we shall always be His little children, and "doubtless" He will always be our Father. The rush of years cannot touch this!

Isaiah 63:16
Hebrews 1:11, 12

Fear not the westering shadows,
    O Children of the Day!
For brighter still and brighter,
    Shall be your homeward way.
Resplendent as the morning,
    With fuller glow and power,
And clearer than the noonday,
    Shall be your evening hour.

TWENTY-NINTH DAY.

The Earnests of More and More.

"He hath given you the former rain moderately, and He will cause to come down for you the rain, the former rain, and the latter rain in the first month."—Joel 2:23.

Deut. 8:2
Joshua 23:14

1 Samuel 12:24
Psalm 103:2

John 13:1
Psalm 71:20, 21
1 Samuel 7:12
Psalm 66:12

Malachi 3:6
Hebrews 13:8
1 Chr. 17:16, 27
James 4:6

Isaiah 26:12

Joel 2:26

Matthew 25:29

Judges 13:23

GOD keeps writing a commentary on His Word in the volume of our own experience. That is, in so far as we put that volume into His hands, and do not think to fill it with our own scribble. We are not to undervalue or neglect this commentary, but to use it as John Newton did, when he wrote—

"His love in time past forbids me to think
He'll leave me at last in trouble to sink;
Each sweet Ebenezer I have in review
Confirms His good pleasure to help me quite through."

The keywords of what the Spirit writes in it are, "He hath," and therefore "He will." Every record of love bears the great signatures, "I am the Lord, I change not"; "Jesus Christ, the same yesterday, *and* to-day, *and* for ever." Every Hitherto of grace and help is a Henceforth of more grace and more help. Every experience of the realities of faith widens the horizon of the possibilities of faith. Every realized promise is the stepping-stone to one yet unrealized.

This principle (and it is a very delightful one) of arguing from what God has done for us to what He will do for us, comes up perpetually in all parts of His word. If He *hath* given us the former rain, it is the pledge and proof that "He *will* cause to come down for us the rain, the former rain, *and* the latter rain"; the blessing already given shall be continued or repeated, and a fuller future one shall be certainly added. Manoah's wife argued well: "If the Lord were

The Earnests of More and More.

1 Samuel 12:24 Ephesians 1:8	pleased to kill us, He would not ... have showed us all these things, nor told us such things as these." Oh consider *what* things the Lord has shown and told you and me! are they not abounding proofs of His purposes towards us? David made frequent use of the thought, arguing from the less to
1 Samuel 17:37	the greater: "The Lord that delivered me out of the paw of the lion and out of the paw of the bear, He will deliver me out of the hand of this Philistine." St. Paul gives a close par-
2 Timothy 4:17, 18	allel, rising from temporal to spiritual deliverance: "I was delivered out of the mouth of the lion. And the Lord shall deliver me from *every* evil work."
2 Cor. 1:10	"Who delivered us from so great a death, and doth deliver; in whom we trust that He will yet deliver us."
Psalm 6:8, 9 Psalm 13:6 Psalm 116:7 Psalm 119:17 Psalm 142:7 Psalm 126:3 Joel 2:21	"The Lord *hath* heard the voice of my supplication; the Lord *will* receive my prayer." "The Lord *hath* dealt bountifully with me," comes first; then follows, "Deal bountifully with Thy servant"; and then, "Thou *shalt* deal bountifully with me." "The Lord *hath* done great things for us, whereof we are glad," leads us on to the prophecy, "Be glad and rejoice, for the Lord *will* do great things."
Numbers 14:19	The same argument is used in prayer. "Pardon, I beseech Thee, the iniquity of Thy people, ... as Thou hast forgiven this people, from Egypt even until now." "Thou *hast*
Psalm 56:13	delivered my soul from death; *wilt Thou not* deliver my feet
Judges 1:15 Isaiah 58:11; John 7:37	from falling?" So in the lovely typical request of Achsah to her father, "Give me a blessing; for thou *hast* given me a south land; give me also springs of water."
Romans 8:32	Turn now to the basis of such expressions of trust and petition. "He that spared not His own Son,"—there is the entirely incontrovertible fact of what He hath done: "shall He not with Him also freely give us all things,"—there is
John 13:1	the inspired conclusion of what He will do. "Having loved His own which were in the world, He loved them unto the
Philippians 1:6	end." "He which *hath* begun a good work in you *will* perform it until the day of Jesus Christ." For how true is the
1 Cor. 3:17 Ephesians 2:21 Zechariah 4:9 Hebrews 3:6	type, both as to each individual temple of the Holy Ghost, and "all the building that groweth unto an holy temple in the Lord:"—"The hands of Zerubbabel have laid the foundation of this house, his hands shall also finish it,"—"His own

house, whose house are we." Our Lord Jesus Christ endorses it in the very amen of His great prayer: "I *have* declared unto them Thy name, and *will* declare it." Only let us simply receive and believe what He shows us and tells us, and then to every Nathanael who comes to Him, He will say, "Because I said unto thee, I saw thee under the fig tree, believest thou? thou shalt see greater things than these." Then we shall have, personally and indeed, "showers of blessing."

Unto him that hath Thou givest
Ever more abundantly;
Lord, I live because Thou livest,
   Therefore give more life to me,
Therefore speed me in the race,
Therefore let me grow in grace.

John 17:26

John 1:50

Ezekiel 34:26

THIRTIETH DAY.

The Perpetual Presence.

"Lo, I am with you alway."—Matthew 28:20.

Psalm 38:6
Job 23:3

SOME of us think and say a good deal about "a sense of His presence"; sometimes rejoicing in it, sometimes going mourning all the day long because we have it not; praying for it, and not always seeming to receive what we ask; measuring our own position, and sometimes even that of others, by it; now on the heights, now in the depths about it. And all this April-like gleam and gloom instead of steady summer glow, because we are turning our attention upon the *sense* of His presence, instead of the changeless *reality* of it!

Isaiah 41:10
Hebrews 13:5

All our trouble and disappointment about it is met by His own simple word, and vanishes in the simple faith that grasps it. For if Jesus says simply and absolutely, "Lo, I *am* with you *always*," what have we to do with feeling or "sense" about it? We have only to *believe* it, and to *recollect* it. And it is only by thus believing and recollecting that we can realize it.

Exodus 3:14

It comes practically to this: Are you a disciple of the Lord Jesus at all? If so, He says to you, "I am with you *alway*." That overflows all the regrets of the past and all the possibilities of the future, and most certainly includes the present. Therefore, at this very moment, as surely as your eyes rest on this page, so surely is the Lord Jesus with you. "I *am*," is neither "I was," nor "I will be." It is always abreast of our lives, always encompassing us with salvation. It is a splendid perpetual "*Now*." It always means "I am with you *now*," or it would cease to be "I am" and "alway."

Psalm 42:5, margin
Acts 18:9, 10
Exodus 33:14

Is it not too bad to turn round upon that gracious presence, the Lord Jesus Christ's own personal presence here and now, and, without one note of faith or whisper of thanksgiving, say, "Yes, but I don't realize it!" Then it is, after all, not the presence, but the realization that you are seeking—the shadow, not the substance! Honestly, it is so! For you have such absolute assurance of the reality, put into the very plainest words of promise that divine love could devise, that you dare not make Him a liar and say, "No! He is *not* with me!" All you *can* say is, "I don't feel a *sense* of His presence." Well, then, be ashamed of doubting your beloved Master's faithfulness, and "never open thy mouth any more" in His presence about it. For those doubting, desponding words were said *in His presence*. He was *there, with* you, while you said or thought them. What must He have thought of them!

As the first hindrance to realization is not believing His promise, so the second is not *recollecting* it, not "keeping it in memory." If we were always recollecting, we should be always realizing. But we go forth from faith to forgetfulness, and there seems no help for it. Neither is there, in ourselves. But "in Me is thine help." Jesus Himself had provided against this before He gave the promise. He said that the Holy Spirit should bring all things to our remembrance. It is no use laying the blame on our poor memories, when the Almighty Spirit is sent that He may strengthen them. Let us make real use of this promise, and we shall certainly find it sufficient for the need it meets. He can, and He will, give us that holy and blessed recollectedness, which can make us dwell in an atmosphere of remembrance of His presence and promises, through which all other things may pass and move without removing it.

Unbelief and forgetfulness are the only shadows which can come between us and His presence; though, when they have once made the separation, there is room for all others. Otherwise, though all the shadows of earth fell around, none could fall between; and their very darkness could only intensify the brightness of the pavilion in which we dwell, the Secret of His Presence. They could not touch what one has called "the unutterable joy of shadowless communion."

The Perpetual Presence.

2 Samuel 7:20

Psalm 23:4

What shall we say to our Lord tonight? He says, "I *am* with you alway." Shall we not put away all the captious contradictoriness of quotations of our imperfect and doubt-fettered experience, and say to Him, lovingly, confidingly, and gratefully, "Thou *art* with me!"

> "I am with thee!" He hath said it,
>   In His truth and tender grace!
> Sealed the promise, grandly spoken,
> With how many a mighty token
>   Of His love and faithfulness!
>
> "I am with thee!" With thee always,
>   All the nights and "all the days";
> Never failing, never frowning,
> With His loving-kindness crowning,
>   Tuning all thy life to praise.

THIRTY-FIRST DAY.

The Fame-excelling Reality.

"Thou exceedest the fame that I heard."—2 Chronicles 9:6.

<small>Psalm 73:25
Revelation 1:5
Galatians 2:20
Isaiah 43:1
Jeremiah 31:3
John 15:26
2 Cor. 4:10
John 14:19
Romans 8:39

1 Kings 10:7

John 1:46
Luke 24:16
Acts 17:27
Hebrews 1:12;
Romans 10:12
John 4:42
1 John 4:14
Job 19:27
John 20:28

Psalm 65:4
Joel 2:26
Jer. 31:14, 25
Psalm 107:9</small>

THOU! Lord Jesus! for whom have I in heaven but Thee? and there is none upon earth that I desire beside Thee. Thou! who hast loved me and washed me from my sins in Thine own blood. Thou! who hast given Thyself for me. Thou! who hast redeemed me, called me, drawn me, waited for me. Thou! who hast given me Thy Holy Spirit to testify of Thee. Thou! whose life is mine, and with whom my life is entwined, so that nothing shall separate or untwine it. "*Thou* exceedest the fame that I heard!"

Yet I heard a great fame of Thee. They told me Thou wert gracious. They told me as much as they could put into words. And they said, "Come and see." I tried to come, but I could not see. My eyes were holden, though Thou wast "not far." Then I heard what Thou wast to others, and I knew that Thou wast the same Lord. But now I believe, not because of their saying, for I have heard Thee myself, and know that Thou art indeed the Christ, the Saviour of the world—my Saviour. Thee, "whom I shall see for myself," I now know for myself; my Lord and my God.

I did not understand how there could be satisfaction here and now. It seemed necessarily future, in the very nature of things. It seemed, in spite of Thy promises, that the soul could never be filled with anything but heaven. But Thou fillest, Thou satisfiest it.

> "Now it wonderingly rejoiceth,
>   Finds in Thee unearthly bliss,
> Rests in Thy divine perfection,
>   And is satisfied with this.

> "Altogether fair and lovely,
> Evermore the same to me;
> Precious, infinite Lord Jesus,
> *I am satisfied with Thee!*"
>
> Jean S. Pigott

cf. John 1:45
with 49–51
Philippians 3:8
Colossians 2:3

For Thou *exceedest* the fame that I heard. I find in Thee more than I heard, more than I expected, "more than all." The excellency of the knowledge of Thee, Christ Jesus my Lord, not only includes all other treasures of wisdom and knowledge, but outshines them all. Every other fame that I heard has had some touch of disappointment; imagination could always flash beyond reality, even if actual expectation, quieted by experience, had kept within the mark. But "now I see" that Thou exceedest all that God-given mental powers can reach; every glimpse is but an opening vista, all the music is but a prelude; what I know of Thee only magnifies the yet unknown. All the God-implanted craving for something beyond, all the instinct for the infinite, is met, responded to, satisfied in Thee. There is no part of my being but finds its full scope and its true sphere in Thee.

John 9:25

Ephesians 3:19
Eccles. 1:8

Thou exceedest all that I heard in every respect. No one could tell me what Thy pardoning love, Thy patience, Thy long-suffering would be to me. No one could tell me how Thy strength, Thy grace, Thy marvellous help would fit into the least as well as the greatest of my continual needs. No one could tell me what grace was poured into Thy lips for me. Thou art *All* to *each* of Thy children; a complete and all-excelling Christ to every one, as if it were only for each one. Thy secret is with each. Thou givest the white stone and the new name which no man knoweth saving he that receiveth it. And if Thou exceedest all that I heard, now and here amid the shadows and the veils, how far more exceeding will be Thy unshadowed and unveiled glory! Lord Jesus, I bless Thee for Thy promised eternity. For I shall need it all to praise Thee, that Thou exceedest the fame that I heard!

Psalm 45:2

Psalm 25:14
Revelation 2:17

2 Cor. 3:10
1 Peter 1:8
Psalm 17:15
Isaiah 33:17
1 Thess. 4:17
Revelation 1:5, 6

Is It for Me?

"O, Thou whom my soul loveth."

O, SAVIOUR, precious Saviour,
    My heart is at Thy feet;
I bless Thee, and I love Thee,
    And Thee I long to meet.
A thrill of solemn gladness
    Has hushed my very heart
To think that I shall really
    Behold Thee as Thou art;

Behold Thee in Thy beauty,
    Behold Thee face to face,
Behold Thee in Thy glory,
    And reap Thy smile of grace;
And be with Thee for ever,
    And never grieve Thee more!
Dear Saviour, I *must* praise Thee,
    And lovingly adore!

POSTSCRIPT.

I AM glad to take this opportunity of inviting my readers to join a Union which is not only very pleasant and profitable for ourselves, but peculiarly valuable as an adjunct to our work among others—the "*Christian Progress Scripture Reading and Prayer Union.*" Our members read one chapter every day in the Old Testament, going straight through; and a short evening reading in the New Testament, in consecutive portions, averaging ten to fifteen verses.

"Well, Miss, as long I *was* reading regular, I thought I might as well read what the others were reading," said a young man-servant, as his reason for joining. "As well!" yes, and much better. To begin with, we ought, every one of us, to be "reading regular." There is no doubt about that! How is any soul to "grow" on one meal a day, or on uncertain and occasional draughts of "the sincere milk of the Word"? Regularly, not only as to constancy, but *as to system.* How much time is wasted in indecision, and wondering what to read next! How many are familiar only with their favourite parts of God's Word, neglecting others almost entirely; thus overlooking many a Royal Commandment, and losing much of His Royal Bounty, and gaining no wide and balanced views of the great field of His truth! How can we be "throughly furnished unto *all* good works," if we do not use God's means thereto—"*all* Scripture" (2 Timothy 3:16, 17)?

And if we are, as we ought to be, reading both parts of His Word regularly every day, why not "read what the others are reading"? Why should you read Galatians when we are reading Ephesians, and Ephesians when we are reading Philippians? Why not "keep rank" with all one's Christian friends and thousands of fellow-members, praying for the same light, the same teaching for them and for ourselves? Why not lie down *together* in the green pastures, instead of scattering all about?

Personally, I believe each will find it a real help to have these assigned portions. It is a reminder to the young or unestablished Christian. It is a guard against desultoriness. It is a counteractive to one-sidedness, and a gentle guide into "the whole counsel of God." It will *not* be found a fetter or a limit. There is, there *should* be, plenty of time for any other Bible study which may attract us.

The Christian Progress Union forms a pleasant bond alike for the near and the distant. It is a connecting link for scattered families and severed friends. It is also a great help to profitable intercourse. The mere fact of knowing that those around have certainly been reading the same chapter, opens the way for questions or remarks or mention of striking verses, which might not otherwise have been ventured on, and thus raises the tone of our household conversation. How few of us realize that we have to give account for our empty table-talk! Constantly, too, it will give opportunity for improvement of even a passing greeting, or enrichment of a quickly written note with a living gem of truth.

Let the servants be "partakers of the benefit." With a little kindly explanation, they are almost invariably pleased to join, and the practical benefit is, perhaps, even greater in the servants" hall than in the drawing-room. Children, too, if old enough to read for themselves, are important accessions. "It is so nice for our little boy and girl to join with us," said a Christian mother; "it may be the means of making them steady Bible-readers for life!" It may be a great blessing in Christian schools. Many are joining. In one young ladies" school about sixty of the pupils are members.

Most especially would I commend it to Christian *workers*. Those who have a settled charge will find that no amount of general exhortations to read the Bible will be as effectual as "Come, join with me!" One lady, after joining herself, obtained some fifty members in about a week from her two Bible classes. This is immediate and definite, and will bring persons to a point. Just try it! Join yourself, first; and then see if it is not a new power and blessing among those for whose souls you are labouring! Do not train them into bad ways by getting them to read only once a day. If you do that, you encourage the comfortable idea that they have done their duty very sufficiently by a chapter at night, while the whole day has been Scriptureless. Aim higher at once, and you will strike higher. There is no power in half measures. It is one of the chief benefits of our Union that it is lifting such numbers out of their easy-going once-a-day reading into a more excellent way. I believe it will be found to be a most valuable parochial agent, and that members will be strengthening the hands of their ministers by bringing it before them in this light. *Very* much might be said on this aspect of the Union, but I must not enlarge here.

For those who have temporary opportunities of special work with souls, it is simply invaluable. It is just what we want to consolidate our work. It is our best legacy to those to whom we have been privileged to be God's messengers of blessing. It is putting them on the rails; putting them in the way of further blessing; giving them something which will be definite and perpetual help in the new path. It will be a delightful link, and a reminder to mutual prayer. It will help them to help each other, and give them something to do in trying to get others to join. Work for our young converts is often a difficulty, but this will give immediate opportunity both for confession of Christ and direct usefulness, and often lead to more.

Now, will you not join us? You may do so by sending your full name and address (stating whether Rev., Mr., Esq., Mrs., or Miss) to the Rev. Ernest Boys, Bengeo, Herts, enclosing a penny stamp. You will receive in return a card of membership, a copy of the Magazine, and other papers respecting the Union. If you are not *quite* sure whether you would like it, send for the papers only, and try it for a month. There need be no hesitation about joining on the idea of its being a sort of vow. If you omit a reading, you have not broken a promise, but you have missed a privilege. You can cease to be a member any day *by returning your card of membership*. Those who cannot read for themselves can have the portions read to them. One of our heartiest members is "no scholar," but his little daughter reads to him.

Christian Progress,[1] the organ of the Union, is well described as "a Magazine of help and encouragement in Christian life, testimony and work." "Its aim," says the editor, "is to encourage believers in the Lord Jesus Christ, in their daily walk amidst the realities of life." Members can send questions relating to practical Christian life and work, or to the interpretation of Holy Scripture; also special requests for prayer. But as *Christian Progress* is more especially suited to real believers and educated persons, the same editor now conducts a second organ of the Union, *Living Waters,*[2] a very attractive little magazine, for more general distribution, containing more evangelistic papers, and suitable rather for our younger friends, those in humbler life, and those who are "lingering just outside the door." Both magazines will contain tables of the readings and special notices to members, so that if they do not wish for both, there can be a choice between them.

In conclusion, let me say to every one of my friends, known and unknown, "Come *thou* with us, and we will do thee good!"

FOOTNOTES

[1] *Christian Progress.* Monthly, price 1d. Edited by the Rev. Ernest Boys, B.A. Published by Bemrose & Sons, 10 Paternoster Buildings, London.

[2] *Living Waters.* Monthly, price 1d. An illustrated evangelistic magazine. Published by Haughton & Co., 10 Paternoster Row. Both may be ordered of all booksellers.

His voyage towards Rome.   THE ACTS, XXVII.   His shipwreck at Melita.

A.D. 62.

a ch.25.12,25.
b chap.23.11.
c He. 1. 14.
d De. 32. 9.
Is. 44. 5.
Mal. 3. 17.
Jno.17. 9,10
1 Co. 6. 20.
1 Pe.2.9,10.
e Ps. 116. 16.
Is. 44. 21.
Da. 3. 17.
6. 16.
John 12. 26.
Ro. 1. 9.
2 Ti. 1. 3.
f chap. 19. 29.
g Ge.19.21,29
h Lu. 1. 45.
Ro.4.20,21.
2 Ti. 1. 12.
i chap. 24. 23.
28. 16.
k chap. 28. 1.
l Ps. 130. 6.
β or, *Candy*.
γ The Fast was on the tenth day of

Paul*a* and certain other prisoners unto *one* named Julius, a centurion of Augustus' band.
2 And entering into a ship of Adramyttium, we launched, meaning to sail by the coasts of Asia; *one* Aristarchus,*f* a Macedonian of Thessalonica, being with us.
3 And the next *day* we touched at Sidon. And Julius courteously entreated*i* Paul, and gave *him* liberty to go unto his friends to refresh himself.
4 And when we had launched from thence, we sailed under Cyprus, because the winds were contrary. See c. 24. 1. n.
5 And when we had sailed over the sea of Cilicia and Pamphylia, we came to Myra, *a city of* Lycia.
6 And there the centurion found a ship of Alexandria sailing into Italy; and he put us therein.
7 And when we had sailed slowly many days, and scarce were come over against Cnidus, the wind not suffering us, we sailed under β Crete, over against Salmone;
8 And, hardly passing it, came unto a place which is called The fair havens; nigh whereunto was the city of Lasea.
9 Now when much time was spent, and when sailing was now dangerous, because the γ fast was now already past, Paul admonished *them*,
10 And said unto them, Sirs, I per-

His shipwreck at Melita.

23 For there stood by me this night*b* the 16.1.7. angel*c* of God, whose*d* I am, and whom*e* I serve, Ex. 21. 5. Ro. 1. 1. Jos. 24. 15
24 Saying, Fear not, Paul; thou must be brought before Cæsar: and, lo, God hath given thee*g* all them that sail with thee.
25 Wherefore, sirs, be of good cheer; for I*h* believe God, that it shall be even v. 44. as it was told me. 16. 17 26. 27. II. 20. 20. 6c 21. 13
26 Howbeit, we must be cast upon a De. 9. 3. certain island.*k*
27 But when the fourteenth night was come, as we were driven up and down in Adria, about midnight the shipmen deemed that they drew near to some country;
28 And sounded, and found *it* twenty fathoms; and when they had gone a little further, they sounded again, and found *it* fifteen fathoms.
29 Then fearing lest they should have fallen upon rocks, they cast four anchors out of the stern, and wished*l* for the day.
30 And as the shipmen were about to flee out of the ship, when they had let down the boat into the sea, under colour as though they would have cast anchors out of the foreship,
31 Paul said to the centurion and to the soldiers, Except these abide in the ship, ye cannot be saved.
32 Then the soldiers cut off the ropes of the boat, and let her fall off.

This is part of Acts 27 in F.R.H.'s Bagster study Bible. Verse 23 "... whose I am and whom I serve."

Manufactured by Amazon.ca
Acheson, AB

17096875R00055